Painless Paper-Piecing

Marjorie Rhine

Editor: Ann Anderson
Copy Editor: Rosalie Cooke
Technical Editor: Joanie Weiser
Design and typography: Ann Anderson and Allison Hooper
Quilt Photography: Harvey J. Raider

Publisher's Cataloging-in-Publication
(Provided by Quality Books, Inc.)

Rhine, Marjorie.
 Painless paper-piecing / Marjorie Rhine.
 p. cm.
 Includes index.
 ISBN-13: 978-0-9714501-1-0
 ISBN-10: 0-9714501-1-0

 1. Quilting--Patterns. 2. Patchwork--Patterns.
I. Title.

TT835.R45 2007   746.46'041
                                  QBI06-600307

Make It Easy® Sewing & Crafts Publishing
A Quiltwoman.com Company
3822 Patricks Point Drive
Trinidad, CA 95570
707-677-0105 Toll Free 877-454-7967 FAX 707-677-9162
www.make-it-easy.com and www.quiltwoman.com

Contents

Dedication

This book is dedicated to my longtime quilting buddy and former co-worker, Julie Fugate, who gave me the opportunity to take my love of quilting "to the next level" and convinced me that I could just do it. By the way, Julie, that quilt we talk about that helped us connect as quilters was in YOUR office. It is official now that it is in print!

Acknowledgements

I now know that it takes a lot of work and support to complete a project of this size. *Painless Paper-Piecing* has been a dream for many years and now it is a reality. My small quilt group, Threadheads, kept me going by asking about the book every time I saw them. I want to thank all my testers who worked through early muddled versions of the patterns and actually made sense of them. Your input was invaluable, so thank you to:

Gail Wiebe, Jan Winter, Susanne Wegert, Ann Anderson, Dot Colna, Laverne Barton, Jo Ann Korzenko, Susan Foster, Susan Ainsworth, Gale Schulz, Dianne McRae and Jan Matsen (also known as Mom).

A most special thanks to Anita Daggett who tested just about everything before it went out to my second level of testers.

I appreciate the help from readers and editors Ann Anderson, Joanie Weiser and Rosalie Cooke. Also I'd like to thank Harvey Raider for the great job he did on the quilt photography.

Thanks to Quiltwoman, Ann Anderson, for having faith in my ability to complete this project.

And last, a special thanks to family members Miriam Urquhart (Grandma), Jan Matsen (mother) and Nancy Palomino (sister) for their moral support as I took on this endeavour, and Randy Rhine (husband) for his understanding when I didn't do the dishes or weed the garden, and I stayed holed up in my computer room for hours.

Introduction

I have had a love-hate relationship with paper-piecing for years.

I love the ease of sewing and the unbeatable precision and accuracy of paper-piecing. Simple or complex, blocks go together with crisp points and clean lines every time.

However, there were many things that I didn't like about traditional methods of paper-piecing. Sewing **on** the paper meant I had to eventually rip it off—creating a mess and sometimes weakening or even pulling out the stitching. Figuring out the size and shape for fabric patches, while I was sewing, was difficult and time consuming and I often got it wrong—tiny stitches to remove, wasted fabric and a destroyed paper pattern! So I made the fabric patches extra large and wasted fabric! Since the fabric was sewn **to** the paper, I could only press seams in **one** direction which meant there were often bulky seams meeting other bulky seams.

But, again, I love the **results** of paper-piecing. When I started designing quilt patterns, many were paper-pieced, so I began developing my own process which simply eliminated many of these issues.

Now, with the Painless Paper Piecing techniques presented in this book, you too can learn how to:

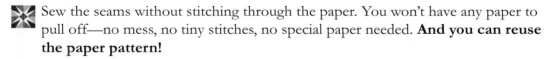

Sew the seams without stitching through the paper. You won't have any paper to pull off—no mess, no tiny stitches, no special paper needed. **And you can reuse the paper pattern!**

Quickly and accurately cut fabric patches with less waste and better control over fabric grain lines and directional prints.

Accurately place the fabric patches onto the paper pattern, **the first time**, assuring coverage of the pattern area and preventing the need to rip seams and re-sew.

Reduce bulk and create seams that you can easily match because you can press seams in any direction, including open.

In the end I hope that you will develop a love-love relationship with paper-piecing as I have.

To benefit most from this book, make sure you read the instructions in their entirety.

The first part of the book walks you, step-by-step, through the Painless Paper-Piecing process. I suggest you start by making the sample block used to illustrate the techniques. Once you understand the techniques, you can apply any or all of them to any paper-pieced project.

The second part has twelve new blocks and twenty projects for your enjoyment.

The paper patterns and general quilting information follow the projects.

Treasure Star Quilt

The book uses the Treasure Star block to demonstrate the Painless Paper-Piecing techniques.

The Painless Paper-Piecing Process

The Painless Paper-Piecing Process is a group of techniques that makes paper-piecing faster, more enjoyable and less wasteful of both fabric and paper. This process helps the quilter eliminate common errors and frustrations associated with traditional paper-piecing and can produce a better finished block and project.

Getting Ready

Previewing the Process

The process is organized into a set of simple steps:

- Assemble tools and create an efficient workspace.

- Understand how to read the paper pattern.

- Mark the master pattern for your project and prepare the paper patterns for sewing.

- Prepare Fabric Cutting Guides.

- Cut all fabric patches before sewing.

- Correctly orient patches before sewing.

- Sew block or sections without sewing on the paper pattern.

- Align sections and seams to complete blocks made with two or more sections.

Finally, I offer techniques on how to:

- make fewer cutting guides for patches that are the same shape

- cut multiple patches at one time

- press seams in the best direction and

- piece patches #1 and #2 using a short-cut.

Supplies

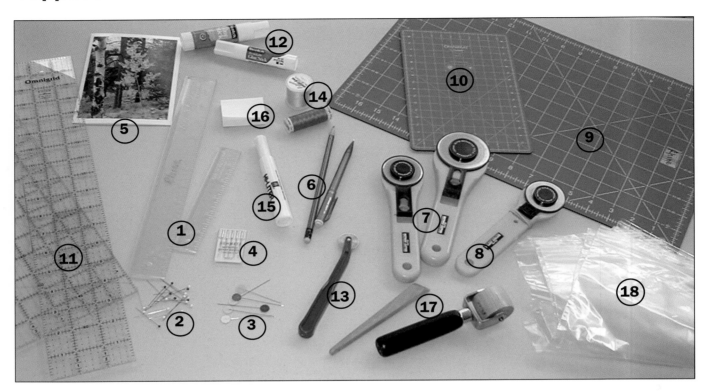

1. **Add-A-Quarter™ rulers, 6" and/or 12"**
   These make trimming the ¼" seam allowances on fabric patches and around the completed blocks very easy and accurate. *The 6" ruler is generally used during the piecing process. The 12" ruler works well for trimming the blocks after piecing.*

2. **Fine sharp pins** hold patches together before sewing.

3. **Flower head pins** secure the fabric patches to the paper pattern after stitching. *The pin's flat head minimizes ruler rocking when a rotary ruler is placed on it..*

4. **Sewing machine needles size 80/12**
   There is no need to use the larger needles recommended in most paper-piecing books.

5. **Lightweight cardboard** makes a good straight-edge for folding paper patterns in preparation for piecing. *A postcard is perfect.*

6. **Pens or pencils**

7. **Rotary cutter with a sharp blade, 45 mm or 60 mm,** for pre-cutting patches and trimming as you sew. *Smaller cutters do not work with the Add-A-Quarter™ rulers.*

8. **Rotary cutter with an old blade** is great for cutting paper patterns. *Paper will dull cutting blades so use an old blade in this cutter. Put a rubber band around the handle to mark it as the paper cutter. Paper scissors can be used in place of a paper rotary cutter.*

9. **Large rotary cutting mat, 18" x 23" or larger,** is needed for pre-cutting patches and trimming blocks.

10. **Small rotary cutting mat, 12" x 18" or smaller,** is very useful next to sewing machine while piecing.

11. **Rotary rulers, 6" x 24" and smaller,** such as 6" square, 6" x 12", 4" x 14" or similar sizes for cutting the various sized strips and pieces needed for the projects.

12. **Scotch® Restickable Glue Stick** is used to secure the first patch to the paper-piecing pattern. *Be sure to buy the* **restickable** *variety. Scotch brand works best. Packaging may be either blue or red plaid.*

13. **Serrated-edge dressmakers' tracing wheel** perforates the stitching lines on the paper pattern. *A smooth-edge tracing wheel doesn't work. I bet you didn't think you would ever use one of these again!!*

14. **Sewing thread to match the most common color in block, 50 weight**
If you are working with light colored backgrounds use a light thread. Dark colored thread might show through the seam after the project is quilted.

15. **Highlighter pen (optional)** works well for marking stitching lines on the back of the paper pattern.

16. **Small sticky notes (optional)** for marking information on pattern and temporarily repairing the paper pattern.

17. **Wooden iron or seam roller (optional)** is an alternative to a full size iron when pressing seams at the sewing machine.

18. **Zippered plastic bags (optional)** are handy for organizing pre-cut patches.

The following supplies are also needed:

Plain, clean paper such as inexpensive copy paper or school notebook paper is best for removing excess ink from photocopied or printed paper-piecing patterns.

A Scrap of fabric at least 9" x 12" provides padding when perforating pattern stitching lines with serrated-edge dressmakers' tracing wheel.

Open-toe presser foot (optional) gives maximum visibility when sewing seams. *A presser foot with a clear plastic insert is also a good choice.*

General sewing supplies and sewing machine

The Workspace

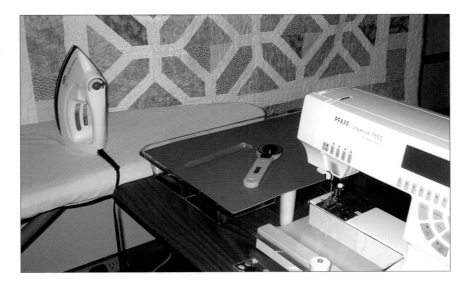

The basic sequence for any paper-piecing project is cut–sew–press, so it is a good idea to make room for comfortable cutting and pressing right next to your sewing machine. I place a small cutting mat on the sewing table immediately to the left of my machine. I also put an iron and ironing board at my left side. My chair swivels so I can easily turn to cut and press as needed. The process of moving between cutting and sewing is easier if you have an acrylic sewing machine table that fits around your machine, or your machine fits into a cabinet with a table level with the bed of your sewing machine.

Sometimes it is not practical or possible to have a full size iron and ironing board right next to the sewing machine for pressing seams as you sew. Alternatives are a mini-iron and small pressing board, or a small pressing tool such as a wooden iron or quilting seam roller. You will still need a full size iron for final pressing of the block after it is pieced.

Understanding Pattern Markings

Painless Paper-Piecing techniques work for any paper-piecing pattern—not just those in this book.

Every paper-piecing pattern is a full-sized pattern for a block or a section of a block.

The example below is for a simple, one-section block, Carrefour. All solid lines on the pattern are stitching lines. These lines outline the *areas* where you will place fabric patches.

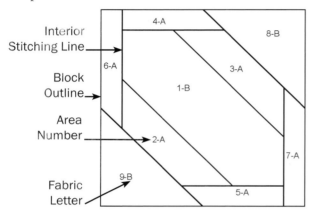

Interior Stitching Lines

Lines in the interior of the pattern are the stitching lines for the fabric patches.

Block Outline

The outside solid line indicates the line for sewing blocks together. Some paper-piecing patterns also have dashed lines ¼" outside the block outlines for the seam allowance around the block or section. In this book, no seam allowances are indicated. You will add the ¼" seam allowances as you trim after sewing.

Area Numbers

Every paper-piecing pattern has a number in each area of the pattern. These numbers indicate the order in which fabric patches are sewn together.

Fabric Letters

Some paper-piecing patterns also include letters for fabric information for each area. This helps make sure you are using the correct fabric for that area.

Pattern Sections

Many blocks are made from several sections which are paper pieced individually, then sewn together to make the block. Sections are usually labelled with *section letters*. Areas within the section are referred to by *section letter* and *area number*, such as X1 or Y3.

The Treasure Star block in this book is made up of five sections. There is one X-Section, two Y-Sections and two Z-Sections per block. In this book, the section number is printed within each area of the pattern. As an example, Z6-D indicates Section Z, Area 6, using fabric D.

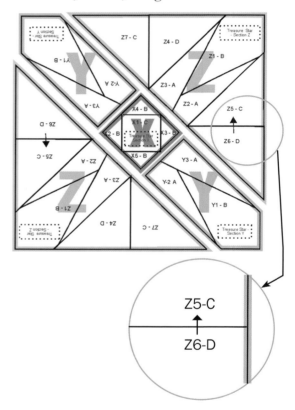

Pressing Information

Some Painless Paper-Piecing patterns have black arrows crossing a stitching line between areas on the pattern. These arrows indicate the recommended pressing direction for the seam.

The Treasure Star example shows the pressing direction for the seam between areas Z5 and Z6.

See *Pressing Seams* on page 28 for more information.

Pieced Unit Patches

Pieced Unit Patches are two or more pieces of fabric sewn together and then treated as a single patch. These patches make it possible to paper piece some blocks that could not otherwise be paper pieced.

A Pieced Unit Patch is indicated by two straight lines crossing a stitching line on the pattern. The area of the Pieced Unit Patch is assigned one number with multiple fabrics indicated.

For example, the Su-Lin (Panda Bear) pattern requires three Pieced Unit Patches. Two of these (X8-AB and X9-AB) are made from a black patch and a background fabric patch. One (X5-BC) is made from one black and two white fabric patches.

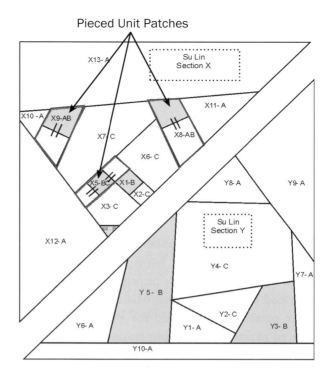

Pieced Unit Patches

Preparing Paper Patterns

In traditional paper-piecing, the quilter sews through fabric and paper on the solid lines of the pattern. This requires a paper pattern for every block. For Painless Paper-Piecing, the quilter does not sew through the paper pattern so one paper pattern can be used for many blocks.

1. Make a fabric "legend"

Make a list of fabrics you will use and choose an easily-recognized letter for each one.

White	W
Purple	P
Red Violet	V
Blue	B

2. Mark fabric letters on the master pattern

Mark each area of the master pattern (the one in this book or your original pattern) with its fabric letter. Either write directly on the pattern or use a "sticky note." If fabric letters are already printed on the master pattern, replace them with *your* fabric letters.

In the following diagram, I've placed yellow sticky-notes with *my* fabric letters over the pre-printed fabric letters.

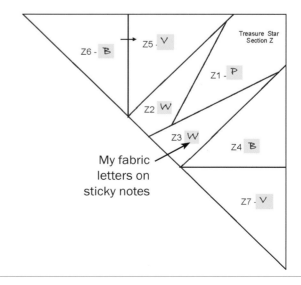

My fabric letters on sticky notes

Preparing Fabric Cutting Guides

For Painless Paper-Piecing, prepare fabric cutting guides before cutting the patches. Using fabric cutting guides assures that the fabric patches are cut to the correct size and shape. The time involved in making the fabric cutting guides is time saved in the patch cutting and sewing process.

Note: Ready-to-use fabric cutting guides for the projects in this book are available on my website. *(See details on page 30.)*

1. Mark the fabric cutting guide

On the pattern copy you set aside for the fabric cutting guide, mark any special fabric positioning requirements such as straight-of-grain or directional-print lines. Use arrows or colored lines.

To avoid bias edges on the finished block, the fabric patches with outside edges of the block should be cut on the straight-of-grain. Use a highlighter pen (in this example pink) to outline the outer edges of the blocks or sections. Patches with only interior stitching lines do not need to be cut on straight-of-grain.

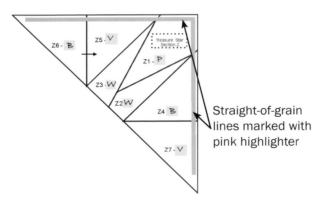

Straight-of-grain lines marked with pink highlighter

2. Cut out block or sections

Cut out the block or sections on the outside stitching (solid) lines. Cut off outside seam allowances on the pattern, if any.

Some blocks may have repeating sections. In this case, **cut out only one** of each of these sections to make fabric cutting guides. In the Treasure Star example, cut one each of Sections X, Y and Z even though there are two X-Sections and two Y-Sections in the finished block.

3. Cut areas apart

Cut apart all areas of the block or section pattern.

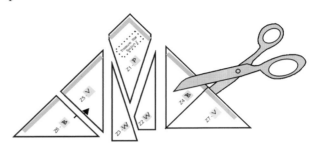

☞*Tip!*

Some areas of a block or section may be the same size and shape. They may be exact copies or mirror images. To save time, make fabric guides only for each unique size/shape. For projects in this book, areas that are copies or mirrors of each other are listed on the page with the paper pattern. Details for making and using fabric guides that are copies or mirrors are on page 26.

4. Glue pattern area pieces to paper

Glue the pattern's area pieces to a piece of plain paper, being careful to leave at least ¾" between the pattern pieces. Draw a line around each pattern piece ⅜" from each edge. These lines are the cutting lines on the fabric cutting guides.

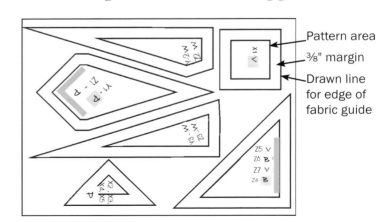

Pattern area

⅜" margin

Drawn line for edge of fabric guide

5. Cut out the guides

Using a rotary cutter and rotary ruler, cut out the fabric cutting guides on the newly drawn lines.

6. Apply glue to fabric guides

Apply restickable—*it must be labeled* **restickable** —glue to the back of each guide so it will not slip when placed on fabric. I have found that Scotch® Brand Restickable Adhesive Glue Stick works best.

7. Sort guides by fabric

Organize the guides by fabric, i.e., all Fabric A guides in one stack, all Fabric B guides in another, and so on.

Note: If you are using one guide for all pattern areas of the same shape, you might want to make a separate stack for the guides that are used for multiple fabrics

Tip!

Do not cut off the points of long, skinny triangular fabric cutting guides or fabric patches. These points will help you properly align fabric patches for sewing.

Pre-cutting Fabric Patches

Pre-cutting fabric patches speeds up the sewing because they are cut to the correct size and shape— no guessing or trial and error while you are piecing.

1. Determine number of fabric patches needed

Choose one of the project's fabrics and select all the guides used for that fabric. Determine the number of fabric patches needed for each pattern area. All projects in this book list the number of fabric patches to cut.

The illustrations that follow use Fabric B—the dark purple fabric from the Treasure Star block.

2. Cut fabric strips to length or width of guide

Paying attention to the straight-of-grain or directional print lines you drew on the fabric cutting guide, place the guide on the fabric. Use a rotary cutter and ruler to cut a strip a little bigger than the guide.

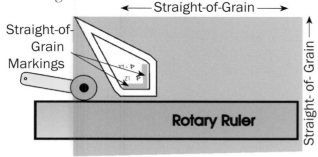

Tip!
I like to cut the patches that need the widest strips first. Any leftover fabric can be used for smaller patches.

3. Cut fabric patches

Place the fabric strip **right side down** on the cutting mat. Lay the fabric cutting guide, **with printed side up,** on the fabric strip and cut around the guide with a rotary cutter and ruler. It is not necessary to cut the fabric patch precisely or to the exact size of the guide, so cutting can go very quickly. You can layer your fabrics to cut multiples of one patch at a time; however, all fabric strips in the stack must be right side down.

Continue until all patches in that fabric are cut for your project.

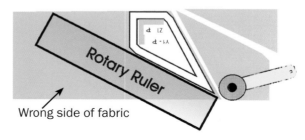

Wrong side of fabric

4. Store patches

Place the fabric patches in a zippered plastic bag labeled with block name, section letter, area number and fabric letter.

Put the cutting guide in the bag with the patches. If you are using guides for copies and mirrors, this might not be possible.

Repeat Steps 1 through 4 for each fabric in the project. The patches are now organized and ready for sewing.

Remember: Some guides can be used to cut more than one patch type. For example, the Treasure Star Block has sixteen patches but only six fabric cutting guides are needed because many of the areas are duplicate shapes (copies or mirrors).

Making Blocks or Sections

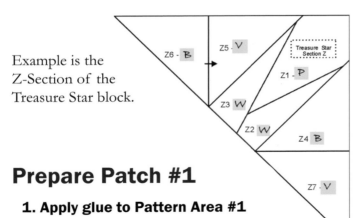

Example is the Z-Section of the Treasure Star block.

Prepare Patch #1

1. Apply glue to Pattern Area #1

Place the perforated paper pattern **printed side down** and locate the perforations that outline Pattern Area #1. Using a **restickable** glue stick, cover as much of area #1 as possible with glue—**do not** apply the glue to the stitching lines or to other areas. Allow the glue to set for a minute, then remove any excess by gently dabbing with a scrap of fabric or paper. If you get glue on the stitching lines or other pattern areas you can rub it off with your finger.

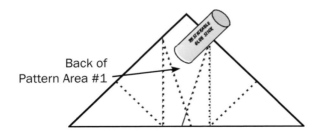

Back of Pattern Area #1

2. Position Fabric Patch #1

Place Fabric Patch #1 **right side down** on the table. Center Pattern Area #1, **printed side up**, over the fabric patch. The fabric patch should extend at least ¼" beyond the outline of the pattern area on all sides.

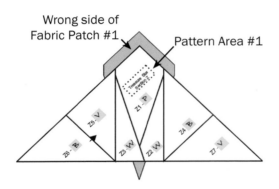

Wrong side of Fabric Patch #1 — Pattern Area #1

Check to make sure that there is at least ¼" of fabric all around Pattern Area #1 by folding the pattern back on all lines around Pattern Area #1.

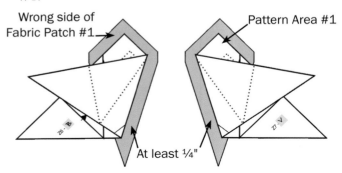

Wrong side of Fabric Patch #1 — Pattern Area #1

At least ¼"

3. Secure patch with pin

Unfold the pattern to show the printed side and secure the fabric to the pattern with a flower head pin. If possible, the pin should not cross any of the pattern stitching lines. Large patches may need more than one pin. Small patches may not need pins.

Line Up the Next Patch

4. Locate next stitching line

The next stitching line will always be the solid line between a fabric patch already on the paper pattern and the next area to be covered. The next stitching line in this example is between Pattern Areas #1 and #2.

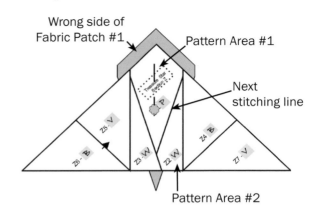

Wrong side of Fabric Patch #1 — Pattern Area #1

Next stitching line

Pattern Area #2

5. Fold pattern back on next stitching line

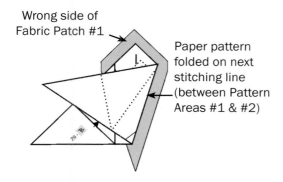

Wrong side of Fabric Patch #1

Paper pattern folded on next stitching line (between Pattern Areas #1 & #2)

6. Trim seam allowance to ¼"

To create the ¼" allowance for the next seam, place the lip of the Add-A-Quarter™ ruler against the paper fold and trim the fabric along the edge of the ruler.

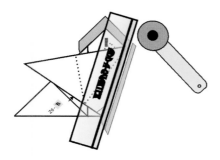

7. Align fabric patch with pattern

On the back of the folded pattern, match the **shape** of Pattern Area #2 to Fabric Patch #2 Position Fabric Patch #2 **right side up** in the same orientation as the pattern area.

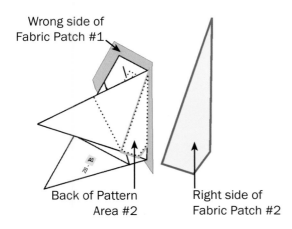

Wrong side of Fabric Patch #1

Back of Pattern Area #2

Right side of Fabric Patch #2

In the example, Pattern Area #2 is outlined in orange and Fabric Patch #2 is outlined in blue.

8. Bring pattern and patch together

Without changing the orientation of either the pattern or the fabric, carefully pick up the pattern/patch unit and place it on top of Fabric Patch #2. Align **right** edge of the fabric attached to the pattern (Fabric Patch #1) with the **right** edge of the new fabric patch. Fabric Patch #2 should extend beyond Pattern Area #2 by at least ¼" on all sides. Fabrics are right sides together.

The following diagrams show two possible placements for Treasure Star Pattern Area #2 onto Fabric Patch #2. The outline of Pattern Area #2 is in orange and the outline of Fabric Patch #2 is in blue. Although Fabric Patch #2 is on the bottom of the stack, its position "shows through" so you can compare it to Pattern Area #2.

This first diagram shows correct placement. Raw edges of Fabric Patches #1 and #2 are aligned and there is at least ¼" of fabric all around Pattern Area #2.

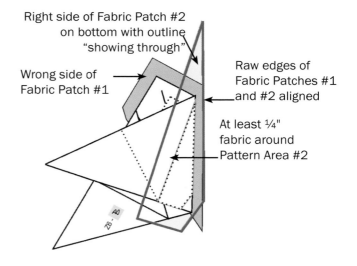

Right side of Fabric Patch #2 on bottom with outline "showing through"

Wrong side of Fabric Patch #1

Raw edges of Fabric Patches #1 and #2 aligned

At least ¼" fabric around Pattern Area #2

In this second diagram, Fabric Patch #2 is shifted too far down and there is not ¼" of fabric at the left of the pattern area. This placement will not work. Fabric Patch #2 fabric needs to be moved up.

With practice, you will be able to determine at a glance whether or not the pattern area is roughly centered over the fabric patch—with raw edges aligned along the seamline to be stitched and with at least ¼" of fabric surrounding the pattern area.

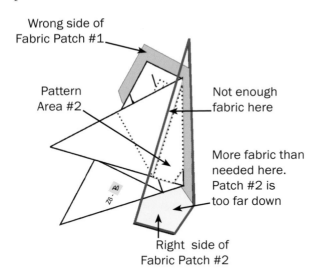

Wrong side of Fabric Patch #1

Pattern Area #2

Not enough fabric here

More fabric than needed here. Patch #2 is too far down

Right side of Fabric Patch #2

☞Tip!

If you have extra fabric along one edge of the pattern area when positioning a patch before stitching, there is probably not enough along another edge and repositioning the fabric is necessary.

☞Tip!

Sometimes, especially with triangles, it is difficult to determine how to orient the patch, i.e., which is the correct edge of the patch to stitch.

With the pattern folded, place the fabric patch, **right side up**, on top of the **back** of the pattern area to be covered. Rotate the patch until the angles of the triangle match the angles on the pattern.

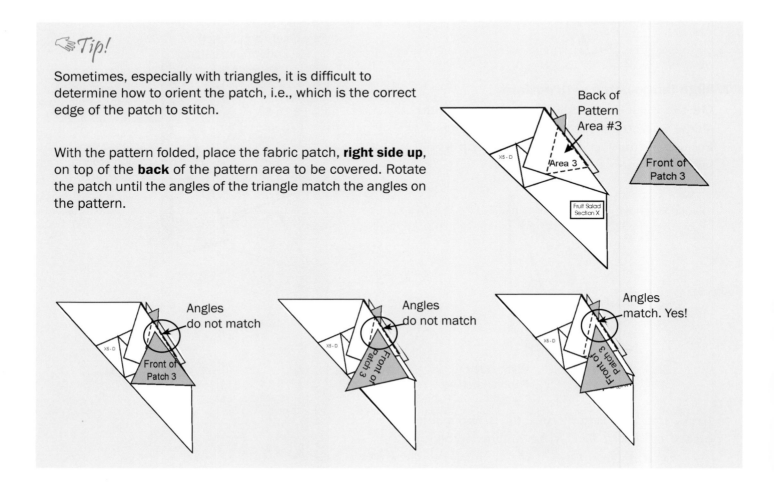

Back of Pattern Area #3

Area 3

Front of Patch 3

Fruit Salad Section X

Angles do not match

Front of Patch 3

Angles do not match

Front of Patch 3

Angles match. Yes!

Front of Patch 3

Sew, Press and Pin

9. Stitch seam

With the paper folded on the sewing line, stitch the seam very close to the paper fold. Start stitching at least ¼" before you reach the folded pattern and continue stitching at least ¼" beyond the folded pattern. The stitch length should be your normal piecing stitch length—usually 2 mm on metric machines and about 15 stitches per inch on non-metric machines.

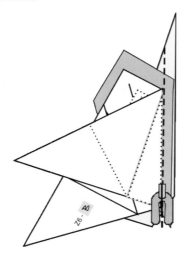

If you catch a little of the paper in the seam it is OK. After the patch is pressed you can gently pull the stitches away from the paper

10. Press seam

Check the pattern for pressing directions. With the pattern still folded, flip the assembly over to the fabric side and press the seam with a hot, dry iron. Press in the direction indicated. Normally you will press the seam toward the patch just added. However, since the fabric is not sewn to the paper pattern you can press the seam in either direction or even open if you wish. See page 28 for more information.

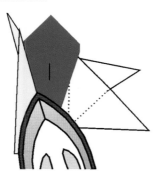

11. Check seam alignment

Flip the assembly back to the paper side and make sure that, after pressing, the stitching is still lined up with the paper fold. If the stitching has moved away from the fold, gently push the fabric and stitching back into alignment.

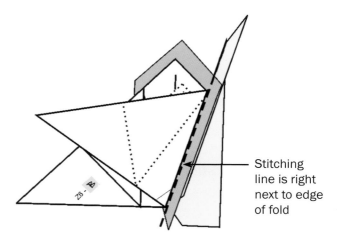

Stitching line is right next to edge of fold

12. Pin patch to pattern

Unfold the paper pattern and secure the paper to the fabric patch with a flowerhead pin. Large patches may need more than one pin.

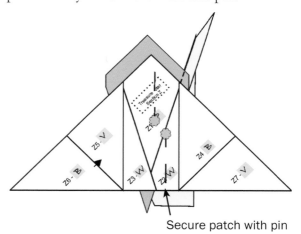

Secure patch with pin

☞Tips!

If the fabric and pattern shift when you pick them up to take them to the sewing machine, lay them back down, correct placement and pin them together in the seam allowance, parallel to the seamline, before you pick them up.

Do all pinning from the paper side of the block. Press only on the fabric side because the heads of the flowerhead pins will melt if they come in direct contact with the hot iron. When the pins are placed on the paper side of the block, the paper and fabric protect the heads from the heat.

Practice #2

Patches #1 and #2 are now sewn. Let's go through steps 4 through 12 again for the next Treasure Star Fabric Patch, #3.

4. Locate next stitching line

The stitching line for Fabric Patch #3 is between Pattern Areas #1 and #3.

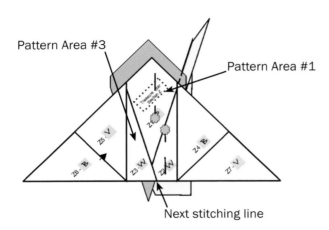

Pattern Area #3

Pattern Area #1

Next stitching line

5. Fold pattern back on next stitching line

6. Trim seam allowance to ¼"

Trim the left edge of Fabric Patch #1 this time.

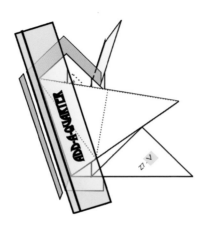

7. Align fabric patch with pattern

The orientation of Fabric Patch #3 matches the orientation of Pattern Area #3.

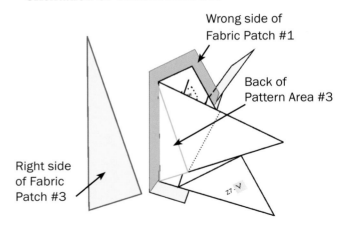

Wrong side of Fabric Patch #1

Back of Pattern Area #3

Right side of Fabric Patch #3

8. Bring pattern and patch together

Fabric Patch #3 extends beyond the pattern area by at least ¼" on all sides.

9. Stitch the seam

Note the assembly is rotated in the diagram to show position for stitching.

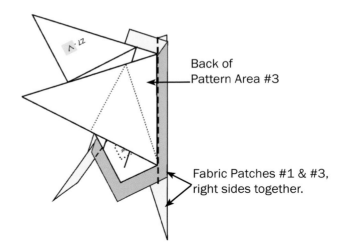

Back of Pattern Area #3

Fabric Patches #1 & #3, right sides together.

10. Press seam

Leave the paper pattern folded and press from the fabric side.

11. Check seam alignment

⚡Caution

As work on the block progresses, keep checking to make sure that patch and fold lines on the pattern still line up with previous stitching lines. If they do not line up, gently push the stitching lines back into alignment and re-pin.

12. Pin patch to pattern

Unfold paper pattern and pin Fabric Patch #3 to the paper pattern.

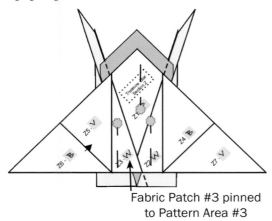

Fabric Patch #3 pinned
to Pattern Area #3

Practice #3

Fabric Patch #3 has been added. Let's do one more to add Fabric Patch #4.

4. Locate next stitching line

The next stitching line is between Pattern Areas #2 and #4.

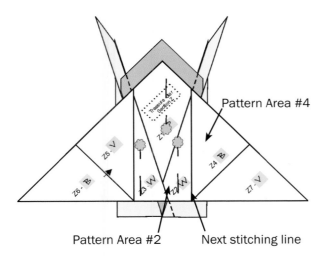

Pattern Area #4

Pattern Area #2   Next stitching line

5. Fold pattern back on next stitching line

6. Trim seam next to stitching line to ¼"

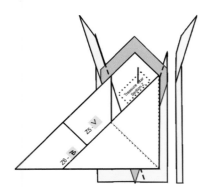

7. Align fabric patch with pattern

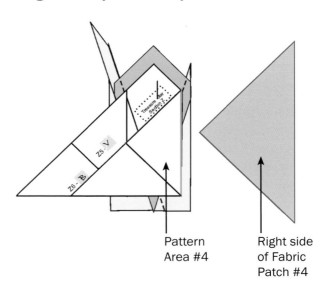

Pattern
Area #4

Right side
of Fabric
Patch #4

8. Bring pattern and patch together

9. Stitch seam

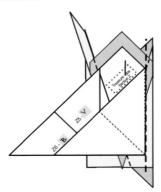

10. Press seam

11. Check seam alignment

12. Pin patch to pattern

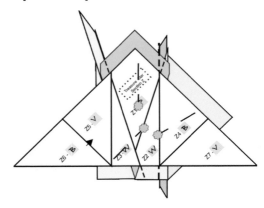

Repeat Steps 4 through 12 until you have stitched fabric patches to all areas.

Finishing Blocks or Sections

13. Press section or block

After adding all patches, give the block one last pressing with a hot iron—on the fabric side! Do not remove paper yet!

14. Trim outside of section or block

With the paper still attached, use the Add-A-Quarter™ ruler to trim around the outside edges of the block. Fit the lip of the ruler snuggly against the edge of the pattern. You must have at least ¼″ of fabric for a seam allowance.

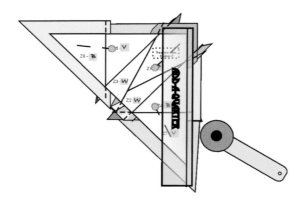

15. Remove the pattern

Remove the pins and separate the section or block from the pattern. The section or block is ready to sew into your project and the paper pattern is ready to use again!

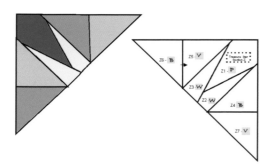

✎Tips!

• After patches are added and secured with pins, you may be able to remove some of the pins from the interior of the block. I usually end up with as many pins in the unit as there are "corners" on the block or section: three pins for a triangle, four for a square, etc.

• Don't trim the block until all stitching for the block is complete.

✎Tip!

If you have trouble with your blocks stretching after you take them off the paper, try stay-stitching ⅛" from the edge of the block or section before removing the pattern.

Sew Remaining Blocks

Repeat the paper-piecing process for all sections and blocks in your project. The Quick Reference Chart below will help you remember the Painless Paper-Piecing steps. If you have been practicing the process with the Treasure Star section, refer to page 32 for completing the block or project.

Painless Paper-Piecing Quick Reference

For adding Fabric Patch #1:
1. Apply restickable glue to Pattern Area #1.
2. Position Fabric Patch #1 on pattern.
3. Secure Fabric Patch #1 with pin.

For adding remaining fabric patches:
4. Locate the next sewing line.
5. Fold pattern back on next sewing line.
6. Trim to ¼" seam allowance.
7. Align next fabric patch with pattern.
8. Bring pattern and fabric patch together.
9. Stitch the seam.
10. Press the seam.
11. Check seam alignment.
12. Pin patch to pattern.

Repeat steps 4 through 12 for the remaining patches in the block or section.

Then continue:
13. Press block or section.
14. Trim outside of section or block.
15. Remove the pattern.

Joining Sections into Blocks

After paper piecing all the sections of a block, you are ready to stitch the sections together. Before sewing, you must line up the sections and match internal seamlines, if any.

Lining Up Sections for Sewing

There are different techniques to use when lining up the sections before sewing. These techniques are based on three different "Patchwork Shapes."

The diagrams that follow show only the basic section shapes and not the seams within the sections.

Patchwork Shape 1

Definition: The "corners" of the two sections match at start and end of the seamline.

This occurs when sewing together, for example, two squares or two triangles of the same size.

To prepare these patches for stitching, match and pin the "corners." Add pins as necessary and stitch using a ¼" seam allowance.

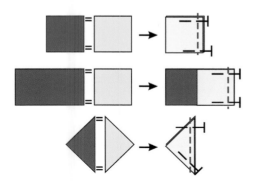

 Tip!

Place the last pin in the seam at an angle (see above) so you can hold onto that pin to help guide the fabric while sewing the last ½" of the seam.

Patchwork Shape 2

Definition: When stitched together, the angled "corners" of the seamline result in either a straight line or squared corner.

Examples are sewing diamonds into a long strip as in a Lone Star quilt, or sewing triangles together into a rectangle.

Prepare for stitching by placing the sections right sides together along the seamline. Adjust the sections until the overlapping sections form a **v** at each end of the seamline. The point of the **v** should be exactly ¼" from the raw edges of the seam. The stitching will go through the middle of the **v**. Pin and sew.

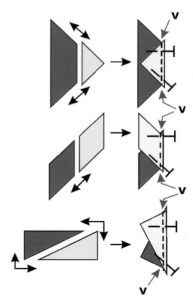

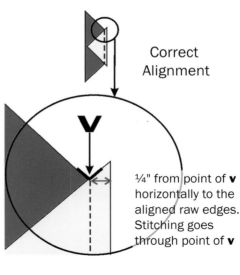

Correct Alignment

¼" from point of **v** horizontally to the aligned raw edges. Stitching goes through point of **v**

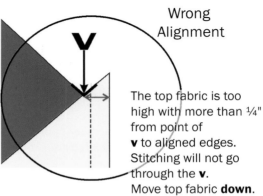

Wrong Alignment

The top fabric is too high with more than ¼" from point of **v** to aligned edges. Stitching will not go through the **v**. Move top fabric **down**.

Patchwork Shape 3

Definition: The "corners" don't match **and** the angled "corners" of the sections do not result in a straight line or squared corner—in other words—anything else that is not Patchwork Shape #1 or #2.

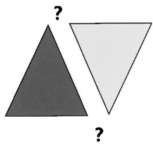

The best way to align these sections for sewing is by lining up the ¼" seam allowance intersections before stitching.

On the wrong side of the fabric, lightly mark dots where the ¼" seam allowances would intersect. Use a non-permanent fabric marking pen or pencil.

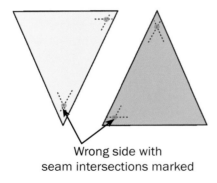

Wrong side with
seam intersections marked

Place the sections right sides together roughly aligning the raw edges along the seamline. Working from the wrong side of one fabric section, push a pin through a seam intersection dot. Push the pin through the second section making sure that the pin comes out at the seam intersection dot. Repeat for the intersections at the other end of the seamline. These are the alignment pins.

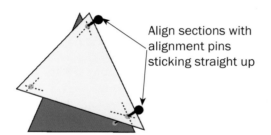

Align sections with
alignment pins
sticking straight up

To secure the sections in the correct seam alignment, hold the alignment pins straight up (perpendicular to the fabric) and place another pin very close to the alignment pin at each end of the seam. Remove the alignment pins. Add other pins as needed to hold the seam in place. Stitch the seam.

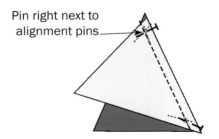

Pin right next to
alignment pins

Mixed Patchwork Shapes

Sometimes the Patchwork Shape at one end of the seam is different from the shape at the other end of the seam. In this situation, use mixed techniques to prepare the seam ends for stitching.

In the example below, the start of the seam will make a straight line (Patchwork Shape 2), while the shapes of the end of the seam are the same (Patchwork Shape 1).

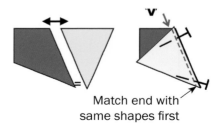

Match end with
same shapes first

First line up the ends that match. Pin, then line up the other end of the seam so the patches form a **v** at the ¼" seamline mark. Pin and sew.

Matching Internal Seamlines

When joining sections together to make a block, you might need to match seamlines within the block. The example below shows internal seams that need to be matched. Line up these seamlines using alignment pins.

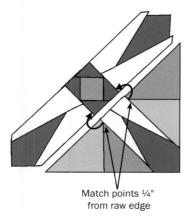

Match points ¼"
from raw edge

With the two sections placed right sides together, poke a pin through the seam on the section on top so that the pin is ¼" from its raw edge. Then poke the same pin through the seam of the section underneath, ¼" from the raw edge. The red arrows point to the match points on the diagram.

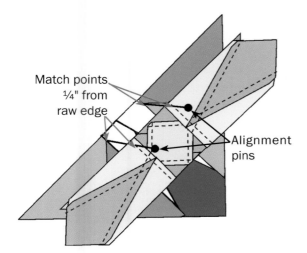

Match points
¼" from
raw edge

Alignment
pins

Bring the sections together so that the alignment pins stand straight up. Secure the alignment by pinning the sections together as close as possible to the alignment pins. Remove the alignment pins before stitching. Be sure to stitch right up to the pins securing the sections together **before** removing them. If you remove these pins too early, seams or edges may be pulled out of alignment.

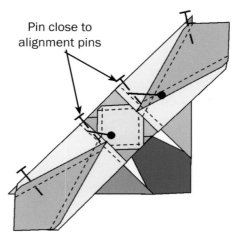

Pin close to
alignment pins

Special Techniques

Cutting Copy and Mirror Patches

Sometimes patches that make up a block are copies or mirrors of other patches in the same project.

- Copies of patches are identical in shape and size to another patch.

- Mirrors or reverse patches are identical in size and shape to another patch but are mirror images or reverses of those patches.

You can save time in preparing fabric cutting guides by identifying patch copies and mirrors and preparing fabric cutting guides only for unique shapes/sizes. These guides can then be used for cutting different area patches at the same time.

To find copies and mirrors, cut out the area pieces for the block and compare them **printed side up**. If areas are exactly the same size and shape, they are copies. If two areas match only when one is turned over, one is the mirror of the other.

The Cathedral Tiles block (page 76) is a good example of a block with patches that can be cut more quickly by using one fabric guide to cut out several patches at a time.

Each Cathedral Tiles block has two sections: one each of Sections X and Y.

 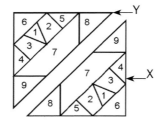

Note: Pattern diagram shows only area numbers. Actual pattern has section and fabric information as well.

For our example, cut the Y section apart on the area lines. You can see that the shape and size of pattern areas Y6, Y8 and Y9 are the same, so they are all copies.

Write the additional pattern numbers Y8 and Y9 on the Y6 pattern area paper and discard the pattern area papers labelled Y8 and Y9.

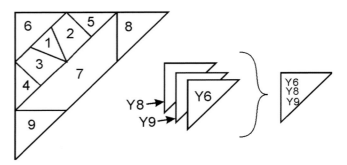

Make a fabric cutting guide from the Y6 pattern area only. Layer fabrics for Y6, Y8 and Y9 together, **all right sides down**. Use the fabric guide for Y6 to cut strips from the layered fabrics. Then use the same guide to cut the strips into triangles.

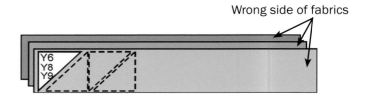

Wrong side of fabrics

Also in Section Y, area Y3 is a mirror or reverse of Y2. The Y2 fabric cutting guide can be used to cut Y2 and its mirror, Y3. Write the additional pattern area number Y3r ("r" stands for reverse) on the Y2 pattern area and discard the guide labelled Y3.

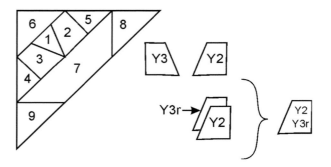

Layer fabrics for Y2 and Y3r **right sides together**—this can be a folded strip if the patches are to be cut from the same fabric. Use the fabric guide for Y2 to cut strips from the layered fabrics and then to cut the strips into patches.

Cutting is done against the wrong side of the Y2 fabric.

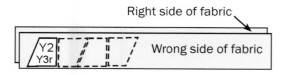
Right side of fabric
Wrong side of fabric
Y2
Y3r

Separate the patches. Patches that are right side down are Y2 patches, patches that are right side up are Y3 patches.

Note: Section Y guides can be used to cut Section X patches as well. Pattern area copies and mirrors are listed on all the paper pattern pages in this book.

Pre-Piecing Patches #1 and #2

If you are making many blocks from the same pattern you can speed up the process by pre-piecing Patches #1 and #2 then adding them to the block as a unit. This is similar to a Pieced Unit Patch.

1. Paper piece Patches #1 and #2 using the paper pattern as described in steps 1 through 9 on pages 16-19.

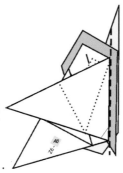

2. Remove any pins and take the paper pattern off the stitched patches. Since the paper is not stitched to the patches, this is easy to do.

3. Using this unit as an example for correct alignment and stitching line placement, select one Fabric Patch #1 and one Patch #2 and put them right sides together. Stitch without the paper.

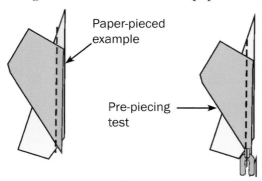
Paper-pieced example
Pre-piecing test

4. To make sure that the second pieced unit is stitched correctly, test it as follows:

• Press the seam in any direction.

• Put the fabric patch unit (#1/#2) right side down on the table. Fold the paper pattern on the first stitching line, the line between pattern areas #1 and #2. Pick the pattern up and align the pattern fold with the stitching line on the pieced unit. Unfold the paper pattern. Fabric Patch #1 should be under Pattern Area #1 and Fabric Patch #2 under Pattern Area #2. Make sure there is at least ¼" of fabric all around the two patches.

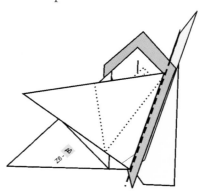

5. If all is well, stitch the rest of Patches #1 and #2 together without the paper pattern. If not, make necessary adjustments in patch alignment and test again before stitching the remaining Patches #1 and #2 together.

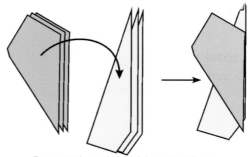
Put patches right sides together and chain piece.

6. To continue sewing the block or section, press and pin the Patch #1/#2 unit to the paper pattern as described in Step # 4 above. Then return to the process of adding remaining patches for the block or section as described in Painless Paper-Piecing steps 4 through 9.

Pre-piecing can be used only for stitching Patches #1 and #2 together.

Pressing Seams

When you are paper piecing the old way, by sewing through the paper, you have only one option for pressing seams—toward the patch just added. Since the fabric is not sewn to the paper when Painlessly Paper-Piecing, you can press seams in either direction or even open. There are several advantages:

- You can create opposing seams on sections or blocks to be sewn to each other, making it easier to "nest" the seams before stitching.

- You can reduce bulk in seams that meet at a match point by pressing them in different directions.

- You can make one patch appear to be lying over the patch next to it (like a flower petal overlapping another petal) by pressing the seam toward the "overlapping" patch.

An arrow that crosses a sewing line on the paper patterns in this book indicates the recommended pressing direction.

- No arrow means that the seam should be pressed toward the patch just added which is the usual direction to press for paper-piecing.

- A single headed arrow indicates that the seam should be pressed in the direction of the arrow, away from the patch just added.

- A double-headed arrow indicates that the seam should be pressed open.

Note: Always press with a hot, dry iron.

Pressing Toward the Patch Just Added

This is the default direction for pressing paper-pieced seams and is the easiest. In the example below, with no arrow crossing the seamline between Pattern Areas #1 and #2, press the seam toward Patch #2 as follows.

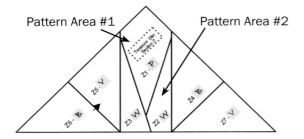

1. Press

After stitching, with the pattern still folded, flip the fabric and paper assembly over to the fabric side and press the seam toward the patch just added, #2 in this example.

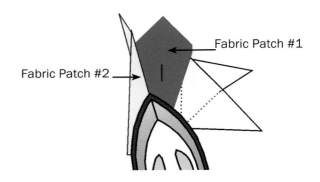

Fabric Patch #1

Fabric Patch #2

2. Check

Flip the assembly back to the marked pattern side and make sure that the stitching is still lined up with the paper fold.

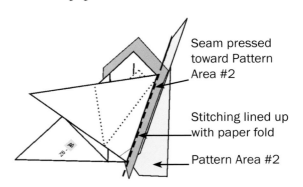

Seam pressed toward Pattern Area #2

Stitching lined up with paper fold

Pattern Area #2

3. Unfold pattern and pin

You are ready to stitch the next seam.

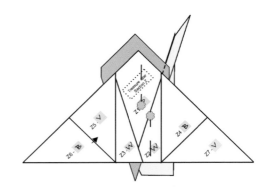

Pressing Away from Patch Just Added

In the example below, the arrow crossing the seamline between areas #5 and #6 indicates that you should press the seam toward Patch #5.

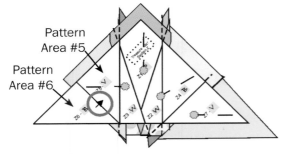

Pattern Area #5

Pattern Area #6

1. Press

After stitching seam and working from the paper side of the pattern with the paper pattern still folded, press the seam **up over** the paper fold. Be careful not to put the hot iron directly on any of the pins.

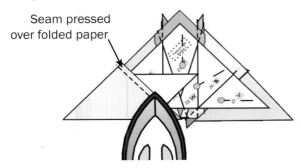

Seam pressed over folded paper

2. Reposition paper and check

Still working from the paper side, carefully lift paper from under the seam and lay it down on top of the seam allowance. Make sure the seam stitching line is right next to the paper fold.

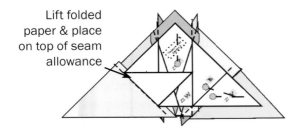

Lift folded paper & place on top of seam allowance

3. Unfold paper and pin.

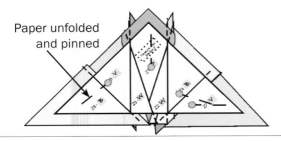

Paper unfolded and pinned

Pressing Seam Open

In this example the double arrow crossing the seamline indicates that the seam should be pressed open.

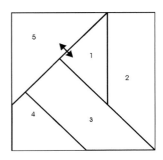

1. Press

With the paper still folded, press the seam open on top of the paper pattern. Take care not to melt the heads of the flower head pins.

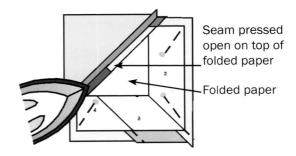

Seam pressed open on top of folded paper

Folded paper

2. Reposition paper and check

Still working from the paper side, carefully lift paper from under the seam and lay it down on top of the seam allowance. Make sure the seam lines up right next to the paper fold.

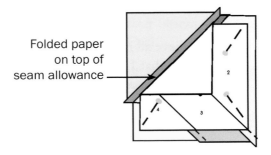

Folded paper on top of seam allowance

3. Unfold paper and pin.

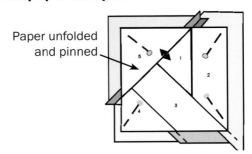

Paper unfolded and pinned

Treasure Star

Wall Quilt 22" x 22"

Marjorie Rhine, 2005, Damascus, Oregon

Treasure Star

Easy

Blocks

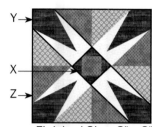

Finished Size: 8" x 8"
Each block has five sections:
one X-Section
two Y-Sections
two Z-Sections

Use lighter or brighter
shades for the baby quilt

Fabric Requirements (In yards unless specified)

Fabric		Description	Wall Quilt 22" x 22" 4 blocks	Baby 38" x 38" 16 blocks
	A	White or Light print	¼	⅞
	B	Dark Purple	⅜	1⅛
	C	Medium Red-violet	¼	⅝
	D	Medium Blue	¼	½
		Border	¼	½
		Binding	¼	⅜
		Backing	⅞	2⅝ vertical seams
		Batting	28" x 28"	44" x 44"

Cutting Borders and Binding

Fabric	Piece	Shape	Wall Quilt		Baby	
			# to Cut	Strip Size	# to Cut	Strip Size
	Border	WOF Strip	2	3½"	4	3½"
	Binding	WOF Strip	3	2¼"	5	2¼"

Cutting Patches for Paper Piecing

Fabric		Patch Name(s)	Total number of EACH in project		
			Block*	Wall quilt	Baby
	A	Y2, Y3, Z2, Z3	2	8	32
	B	X2, X3, X4, X5	1	4	16
		Y1, Z1	2	8	32
	C	X1	1	4	16
		Z5, Z7	2	8	32
	D	Z4, Z6	2	8	32

*Use if you want to make only one block as a way of learning the Painless Paper-Piecing process. The Treasure Star block is used throughout the book to illustrate the techniques.

Making the Blocks (Numbers for Baby quilt in parentheses)

Piecing the Sections

Painlessly Paper-Piece four *(sixteen)* X-Sections, eight *(thirty-two)* Y-Sections, and eight *(thirty-two)* Z-Sections. Follow the recommended pressing direction between patches Z5 and Z6 (shown by arrows on paper pattern) to get opposing seams when sewing the blocks together.

Sewing the Sections into Blocks

Sew Y-Sections to opposite sides of an X-section. Press seams toward the center.

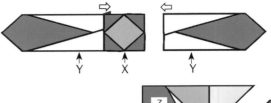

Matching seams as shown in diagram, sew Z-Sections to opposite sides of an X/Y unit. Press seams toward the center. Make 4 *(16)* blocks.

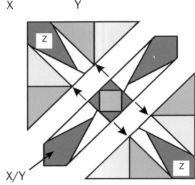

Assembling the Quilt Top

Sewing the Block Rows

Sew blocks into two *(four)* rows of two *(four)* blocks, matching seams as show in diagram below.

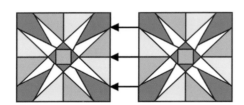

Press seams in adjacent rows in opposite directions. This will result in opposing seams when sewing rows together.

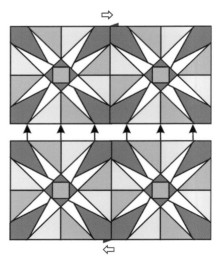

Sewing the Rows Together

Matching seams as shown in diagram above, sew block rows together. Press seams either up or down.

Adding Border

Sew Border strips to the sides. Press seams toward Border. Sew Border strips to the top and bottom of the quilt. Press toward Border.

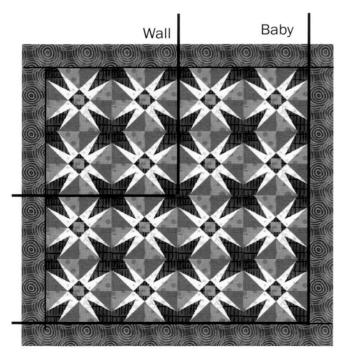

Carrefour

Throw 63" x 77"

Marjorie Rhine, 2005, Damascus, Oregon

Carrefour   Easy

Blocks

Finished Size: 7" x 7"

Fabric Requirements (In yards unless specified)

Fabric	Description	Throw 63" x 77" 48 blocks	Queen 85" x 92" 72 blocks
A	Black for Blocks & Borders	3¾	5⅞
B	Various Prints Scrappy or coordinated	3 yd or 12 FQ* or 48 9" x 10" rectangles	4 yd or 16 FQ* or 72 9" x 10" rectangles
	Binding	⅝	¾
	Backing	4¾ vertical seams	7¾ horizontal seams
	Batting	69" x 83"	91" x 98"

Cutting Strips, Borders and Binding

Fabric	Piece	Shape	Throw		Queen	
			# to Cut	Strip Size	# to Cut	Strip Size
A	Border 1	WOF Strip	6	2½"	7	3½"
	Border 3	WOF Strip	7	5½"	10	8½"
B*	Border Bricks	3½" x 4"	74	**See Fabric B Cutting Note	90	**See Fabric B Cutting Note
	Border Cornerstone	4" x 4"	4		4	
	Binding	WOF Strip	8	2¼"	10	2¼"

Cutting Patches for Paper Piecing

Fabric	Patch Name(s)	Total number of EACH in quilt	
		Throw	Queen
A	2, 3, 4, 5, 6, 7	48	72
B	1, 8, 9	48	72

* FQ means Fat Quarter

**Fabric B Cutting Note

For the scrappy look, you need only a few patches from each print. Fat Quarters or quarter yard cuts can be cut into 9" x 10" rectangles. Patches 1, 8, 9 and either two border bricks or one brick and one border cornerstone, can be cut from one rectangle as shown in diagram to the right.

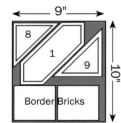

Making the Blocks (Numbers for Queen quilt in parentheses)

Piecing the Sections

Painlessly Paper-Piece forty-eight *(seventy-two)* blocks. As you are piecing the blocks, choose random print fabrics for patches 1, 8 and 9.

Assembling the Quilt Top

Sewing the Block Rows

Arrange blocks as desired in eight *(nine)* rows of six *(eight)* blocks each. Make sure that the blocks in each row "point" in alternating directions. Odd-numbered rows start with right pointing blocks, and even-numbered rows start with left pointing blocks—see diagram below. Sew blocks together into rows. The black arrows between blocks in the diagram below show the seams that need to match as you sew the blocks into rows. Press seams in adjacent rows in opposite directions.

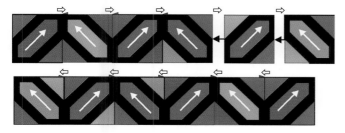

Sewing the Rows Together

Sew block rows together. The black arrows show seams that need to match. Press row seams up or down.

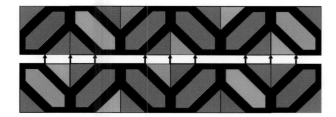

Adding Border 1

Sew Border 1 strips to the sides. Press seams toward Border 1. Sew strips to the top and bottom of the quilt. Press toward Border 1.

Preparing and Adding the Pieced Border

Sew twenty *(twenty-three)* border bricks together to make one long strip. *Important:* the seam will be on the long (4") side of the bricks. Measure quilt from top to bottom. If brick border is too long, trim both ends of border to make it fit. If brick border is too short, add a brick and trim to fit. Make two border strips for sides of quilt but do not sew to quilt yet.

Sew fifteen *(twenty)* border bricks together to make one long strip. Measure quilt from side to side. If brick border is too long, trim both ends of border to make it fit. If brick border is too short, add a brick and then trim to fit. Add 4" print cornerstone squares to each end of the strip. Make one border strip for quilt top and one for bottom.

Sew side borders to the sides of quilt. Press toward Border 1. Sew top and bottom borders to quilt top. Press toward Border 1.

Adding Border 3

Add Border 3 as for Border 1. Press toward Border 3.

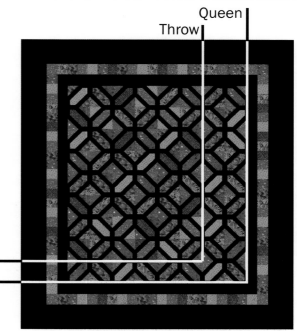

Starflower

Wall Quilt 49" x 49"
Marjorie Rhine, 2005,
Damascus, Oregon

Susan Ainsworth, 2006, Gresham, Oregon

Tablerunner 22" x 58"

Starflower

Blocks

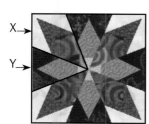

Finished Size: 12" x 12"
Each block has
eight sections:
four X-sections and
four Y-sections

For a lovely Poinsettia
quilt or tablerunner,
make the Starflower
block using Christmas
reds, pinks or whites

Fabric Requirements (In yards unless specified)

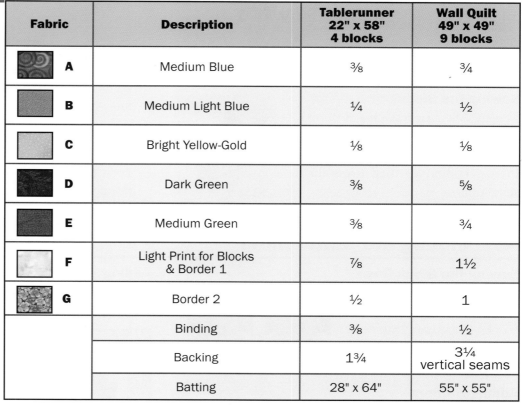

Fabric		Description	Tablerunner 22" x 58" 4 blocks	Wall Quilt 49" x 49" 9 blocks
	A	Medium Blue	3/8	3/4
	B	Medium Light Blue	1/4	1/2
	C	Bright Yellow-Gold	1/8	1/8
	D	Dark Green	3/8	5/8
	E	Medium Green	3/8	3/4
	F	Light Print for Blocks & Border 1	7/8	1 1/2
	G	Border 2	1/2	1
		Binding	3/8	1/2
		Backing	1 3/4	3 1/4 vertical seams
		Batting	28" x 64"	55" x 55"

Cutting Borders and Binding

Fabric		Piece	Shape	Tablerunner		Wall Quilt	
				# to Cut	Strip Size	# to Cut	Strip Size
	F	Border 1	WOF Strip	4	2"	4	2"
	G	Border 2	WOF Strip	4	4"	5	5 1/2"
		Binding	WOF Strip	5	2 1/4"	6	2 1/4"

Cutting Patches for Paper Piecing

Fabric		Patch Name	Total number of EACH in quilt	
			Tablerunner	Wall Quilt
	A	X1	16	36
	B	Y1	16	36
	C	Y2	16	36
	D	Y3	16	36
		Y4	16	36

Fabric		Patch Name	Total number of EACH in quilt	
			Tablerunner	Wall Quilt
	E	X2	16	36
		X3	16	36
	F	X4	16	36
		X5	16	36

Making the Blocks (Numbers for Wall quilt in parentheses)

Piecing the Sections

Painlessly Paper-Piece sixteen *(thirty-six)* X-Sections and sixteen *(thirty-six)* Y-Sections.

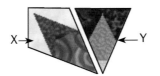

Sewing the Blocks

Sew an X-Section to each Y-Section to make an X/Y unit. There are no seams to match when sewing these sections together. Press the seam open.

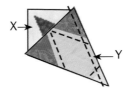

☞ *Tip!*

To properly align X- and Y-Sections before sewing, place a Y-Section on top of an X-Section with points and long edges of the sections aligned. Pin the two sections together at the point to keep them in place. Stitch from the edge of the sections toward the point.

Sew four X/Y units together to make a block. Press seam open. Make four *(nine)* blocks.

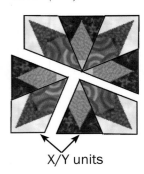

X/Y units

Assembling the Tablerunner

Sewing the Block Rows

Matching seamlines (see black arrows), sew four blocks together into one row. Press seams open.

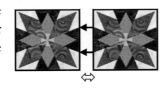

Adding Borders

Sew Border 1 strips to the long sides of tablerunner. Press seams toward Border 1. Sew Border 1 strips to short sides. Press toward Border 1.

Adding Border 2

Add Border 2 as for Border 1. Press toward Border 2.

Assembling the Wall Quilt

Sewing the Block Rows

Matching block seams as shown in tablerunner, sew blocks together into three rows of three blocks each.

Sewing the Rows Together

Matching block seams and seams within each block, sew the rows together. Press seams open.

Adding Border 1

Sew Border 1 strips to the sides. Press seams toward Border 1. Sew strips to the top and bottom of the quilt. Press toward Border 1.

Adding Border 2

Add Border 2 as for Border 1. Press toward Border 2.

Summer Sun and
Summer Moon

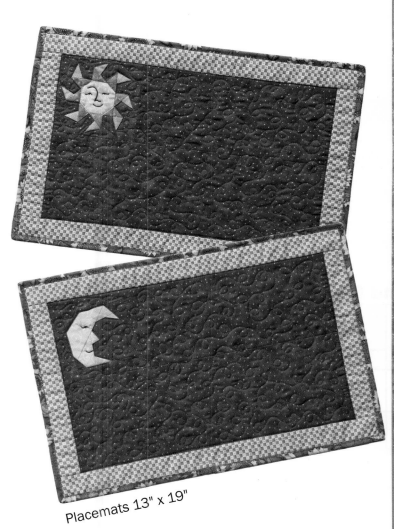

Placemats 13" x 19"

Tablerunner 20" x 44"
Marjorie Rhine, 2006, Damascus, Oregon

Making Four Placemats (Two Suns and Two Moons)

Paper Piecing Moon Blocks and Sun Sections

Painlessly Paper-Piece two Moon Blocks and set aside.

For the 5" Sun Block, Painlessly Paper-Piece two T-Sections, eight U-Sections and eight V-Sections.

Assembling the Sun Block

Sew a V-Section to the top and bottom of each U-Section matching the seam (see black arrow in diagram). Press seams away from center section. Make four side units—two per block.

Sew a U-Section to the top and bottom of each T-Section, matching seams as indicated. Press seams toward center. Make two center units.

Sew a side unit to each side of each center unit, matching seams as indicated. Press seams toward center. Make three blocks.

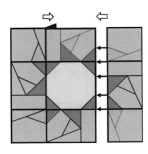

Assembling the Placemats

Sew a 5½" x 12" Background Patch to the right of a Sun or Moon Block. Press toward Background Patch.

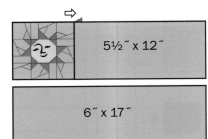

Sew a 6" x 17" Background Patch to the bottom of the Sun or Moon unit. Press toward Background Patch.

Repeat for second Sun and Moon Blocks.

Adding Borders

Sew Border strips to sides of the placemat. Press seams toward Border. Then, sew Border strips to the top and bottom. Press toward the Border. Make four.

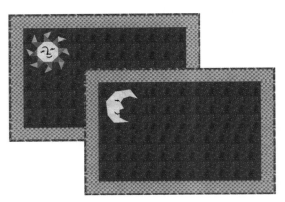

Adding faces to Summer Sun & Summer Moon

Three options:

1. Trace the reverse of the facial features onto the paper side of fusible web and then fuse web to solid black fabric. Cut the features out on the traced lines. Remove the paper backing and fuse to the sun or moon block. If the project is to be washed, stitch the features down with a narrow zigzag or decorative stitch. See manufacturer's instructions for using their product.

2. Using a light box or other light source, lightly trace the face onto the right side of the Sun or Moon Block. Either hand embroider with black thread or use your sewing machine to free-motion embroider the features. Refer to your sewing machine manual for more information.

3. My favorite way to add these faces is to use a Sulky® Iron-on Transfer pen to trace the reverse outline of the eyes, nose, and/or mouth onto plain paper. Use a hot iron to press the paper (ink side down) onto the right side of the Sun or Moon Block. Be sure to test this process before trying it on a finished block! Use a fine tip black fabric marker (I like the Marvy® Extra Fine Tip marker) to fill in the outline. See pen and marker instructions on how to use these products.

Fruit Salad

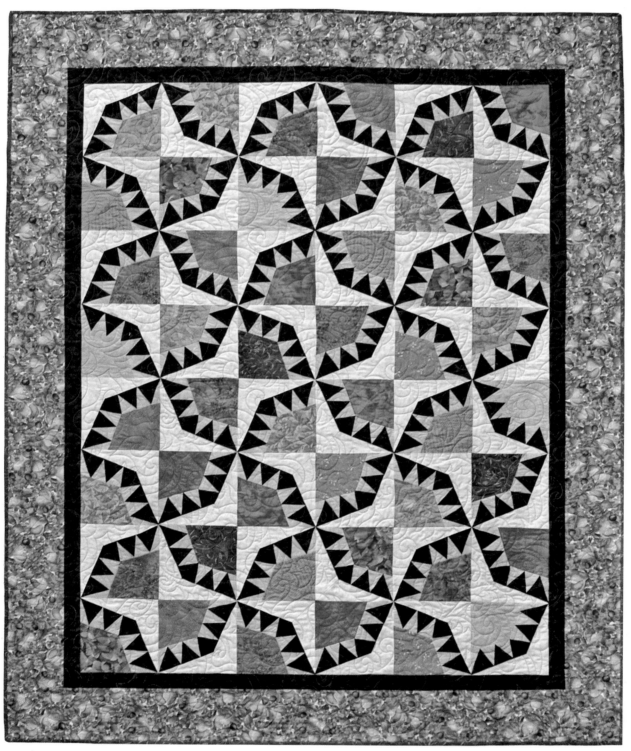

Throw 56" x 70"

Marjorie Rhine, 2005, Damascus, Oregon

Fruit Salad Intermediate

Blocks

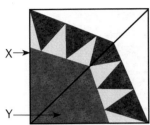

Finished Size: 7" x 7"
Each block has
two sections.

Fabric Requirements (In yards unless specified)

Fabric	Description	Throw 56" x 70" 48 blocks	Twin 70" x 84" 63 blocks
A	Various tone-on-tone prints	Minimum 8 FQ	Minimum 10 FQ
B	Light print	1⅜	1⅝
C	Light yellow	1¼	1½
D	Dark purple for blocks & accent Border 1	1¾	2½
E	Print for Border 2	1⅛	2¼
	Binding	⅝	⅝
	Backing	3⅝ horizontal seams	5⅛ vertical seams
	Batting	62" x 76"	76" x 90"

Cutting Borders and Binding

Fabric	Piece	Shape	Throw		Twin	
			# to Cut	Strip Size	# to Cut	Strip Size
D	Border 1	WOF Strip	6	2½"	7	3"
E	Border 2	WOF Strip	6	5½"	8	8½"
	Binding	WOF Strip	8	2¼"	9	2¼"

Cutting Patches for Paper Piecing

Fabric	Patch Name(s)	Total number of EACH in quilt	
		Throw	Twin
A	X8, Y8	48	63
B	X7, Y7	48	63
C	X2, X3, X6 Y2, Y3, Y6	48	63
D	X1, X4, X5, Y1, Y4, Y5	48	63

Making the Blocks (Numbers for Twin quilt in parentheses)

Piecing the Sections

Painlessly Paper-Piece forty-eight *(sixty-three)* X-Sections and forty-eight *(sixty-three)* Y-Sections.

Note: Pay attention to the arrows for recommended pressing direction between patches Y5 and Y6. This results in opposing seams when you sew the blocks together.

Sewing the Blocks

Sew an X-Section to a Y-Section matching seams as shown in diagram. Press seam open. Make forty-eight *(sixty-three)* blocks.

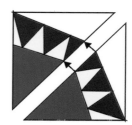

Assembling the Quilt Top

Sewing the Block Rows

Referring to quilt picture, lay blocks out in eight *(nine)* rows of six *(seven)* blocks each. Make sure that the "center" portion of each block "points" in the direction indicated by white arrows on the diagram below. Odd-numbered row blocks point to the right. Even-numbered row blocks point to the left. Blocks within a row alternate between pointing down and pointing up.

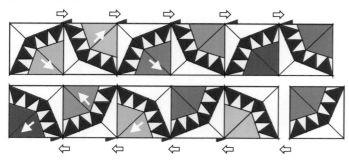

Sew blocks together into rows. Press seams in alternate rows in the opposite direction to make opposing seams when sewing rows together.

Sewing Rows Together

Sew rows together matching seams as indicated by black arrows below. Press seams up or down.

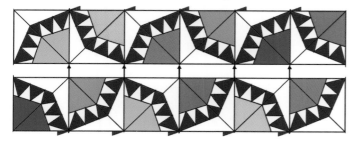

Adding Border 1

Sew Border 1 strips to the sides. Press seams toward Border 1. Sew strips to the top and bottom of the quilt. Press toward Border 1.

Adding Border 2

Add Border 2 as for Border 1. Press toward Border 2.

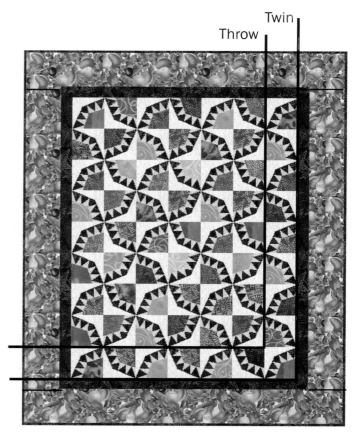

Fruit Salad—a different look...

Instead of a mixed fruit salad quilt try using pinks, reds and greens to make a refreshing watermelon quilt.

Get Set for Christmas

Placemats 13" x 18"

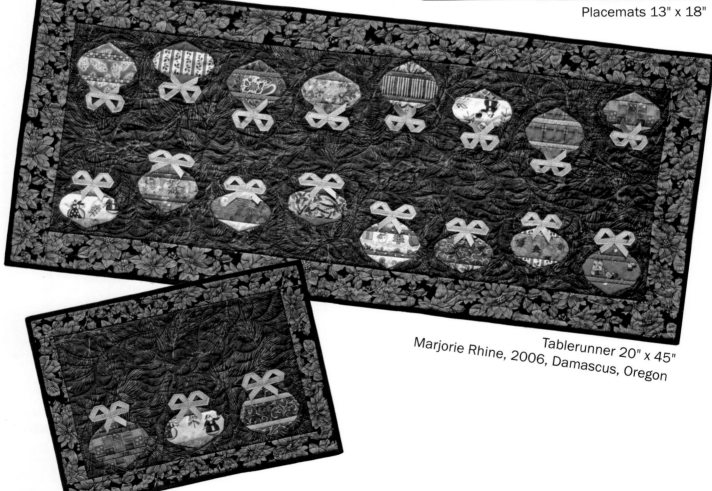

Tablerunner 20" x 45"
Marjorie Rhine, 2006, Damascus, Oregon

Get Set for Christmas Intermediate

Blocks

Block X
Finished Size: 4" x 5"

Block Y
Finished Size: 4" x 5"

Fabric Requirements (In yards unless specified)

Fabric		Description	Tablerunner 20" x 45" 8 X-Blocks 8 Y-Blocks	4 Placemats 13" x 18" 6 X-Blocks 6 Y-Blocks
	A	Green for block background	1⅜	1⅛
	B	Various Christmas Prints for ornament bulb	scraps	scraps
	C	Various Christmas Prints for ornament accent	scraps	scraps
	D	Christmas Print for border	½	½
		Binding	⅜	⅝
		Backing	1½	1¼
		Batting	26" x 51"	34" x 44"

Cutting Backgrounds, Borders and Binding

Fabric	Piece	Shape	Tablerunner		4 Placemats	
			# to Cut	Strip Size	# to Cut	Strip Size
A	Background Sashing Strip	Rectangle	1	3½" x 40½" might need to be pieced from 2 strips	4 pieces @ 6½" x 15½"	2 strips @ 6½" x WOF
	Spacing Patches	2½" x 5½"	10 from 1 strip*	5½"	n/a	n/a
	Spacing Patches	1½" x 5½"	12 from 1 strip*	5½"	n/a	n/a
D	Border	WOF Strip	4	3"	7	2"
	Binding	WOF Strip	4	2¼"	8	2¼"

*First cut the WOF strips then cut the number of background patches indicated.

Cutting Patches for Paper Piecing

Fabric		Patch Name(s)	Total number of EACH in quilt	
			Tablerunner	4 Placemats
	A	X6, X7, X8, X9, X10, X11, X12, X13, X14, X15, X16, X17	8	6
		Y4, Y5, Y6, Y7, Y8, Y9, Y10, Y11, Y12, Y13, Y14, Y15	8	6
	B**	X1, X4, X5, Y1	8	6
	C**	X2, X3, Y2, Y3	8	6

**Coordinate B & C ornament bulb fabrics for each block. Keep cut patches for each ornament together.

Making the Tablerunner

Making the Blocks
Painlessly Paper-Piece eight X-Blocks and eight Y-Blocks.

Adding Spacing Patches
Mix the X-Blocks and Y-Blocks together and choose ten. Choose some of each but it does not need to be half and half. Sew 2½" x 5½" Spacing Patches to the top of five of the blocks and to the bottom of the other five blocks. Press toward Spacing Patches.

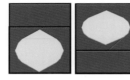

Make 5 of each

Sew 1½" x 5½" Spacing Patches to the top **and** bottom of the remaining six blocks. Press toward Spacing Patches.

Make 6

Sewing the Rows
Sew blocks together randomly in two rows of eight blocks each. Press seams to one side. Sew one row to each side of the long Sashing Strip. Press toward sashing.

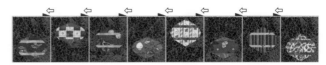

Adding the Border
Sew Border strips to long sides. Press toward Border. Then sew Border strips to short sides of tablerunner. Press toward Border.

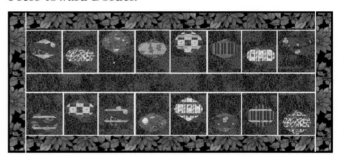

Making Four Placemats

Making the Blocks
Painlessly Paper-Piece six X-Blocks and six Y-Blocks.

Sewing the Block Rows
Sew blocks in rows of three blocks each (four separate rows). Press seams to one side.

Assembling the Placemats
Sew a Sashing Strip to top of each row of ornament blocks. Press toward sashing.

Sew Border strips to sides. Press seams toward Border. Sew Border strips to the top and bottom of the placemat. Press toward the Border. Make four placemats.

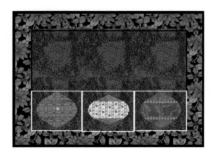

☜Tip! Optional Embellishment

After your project is quilted, add bows to each ornament. Fold a 10" piece of washable ribbon into a bow—don't tie a knot. Flatten the bow and position at the top of an ornament. Stitch first through the bow center then around the outer edge of the bow. Be sure to back stitch at the start and end of the stitching.

Cathedral Tiles

Throw 60½" x 75½"

Marjorie Rhine, 2005, Damascus, Oregon

Cathedral Tiles   Intermediate

Blocks

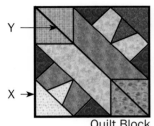

Quilt Block
Finished size
7½" x 7½"
Each block has two
sections: one Section X
and one Y

Border Block
Finished Size
2" x 7½"

Fabric Requirements (In yards unless specified)

Fabric		Description	Throw 60½" x 75½" 48 blocks	Queen 79½" x 94½" 80 blocks
	A	Off White	⅝	⅞
	B	Brick Red	⅝	⅞
	C	Medium Tan Floral for blocks and Borders 2 & 4	2⅝	3¼
	D	Medium Tan Plaid or Print	⅝	1
	E	Light Tan	1⅜	2
	F	Medium Green	1⅜	2
	G	Dark Green for blocks, Border 1 & Pieced Border Cornerstones	1⅞	2½
		Binding	⅝	¾
		Backing	4¾ vertical seams	7¼ horizontal seams
		Batting	67" x 82"	86" x 101"

Cutting Borders, Cornerstones and Binding

Fabric	Piece	Shape	Throw		Queen	
			# to Cut	Strip Size	# to Cut	Strip Size
C	Border 2	WOF Strip	7	3¼"	8	3¼"
C	Border 4	WOF Strip	7	2½"	9	4½"
G	Border 1	WOF Strip	6	1½"	8	1½"
G	Pieced Border Cornerstones	2½" square	4	n/a	4	n/a
	Binding	WOF Strip	8	2¼"	10	2¼"

Cutting Patches for Paper Piecing

Fabric	Patch Name(s)	Total number of EACH in quilt	
		Throw	Queen
A	X1, X6	48	80
B	Y1, Y6	48	80
C	X8, Y9	48	80
C	Z2, Z4, Z6	32	40
D	X9, Y8	48	80

Fabric	Patch Name(s)	Total number of EACH in quilt	
		Throw	Queen
E	X7, Y2, Y3	48	80
F	X2, X3, Y7	48	80
G	X4, X5, Y4, Y5	48	80
G	Z1, Z7	32	40
G	Z3, Z5	32	40

Making the Blocks (Numbers for Queen Quilt in parentheses)

Piecing the Sections

Painlessly Paper-Piece forty-eight *(eighty)* X-Sections and forty-eight *(eighty)* Y-Sections. Follow the recommended pressing direction (see arrows on paper patterns) for patches X9 and Y9 to make opposing seams when sewing the blocks together.

Sewing the Blocks

Sew an X-Section to a Y-Section matching seams as shown in diagram. Press seams open. Make forty-eight *(eighty)* blocks.

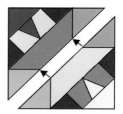

Assembling the Quilt Top

Sewing the Block Rows

Referring to diagram (lower right corner), lay blocks out in eight *(ten)* rows of six *(eight)* blocks each. Make sure blocks "point" in the direction indicated by white arrows in the diagram to the right. Blocks within a row alter-

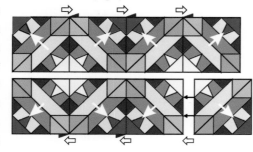

nate between pointing left and pointing right. Odd-numbered row blocks point "up" and even-numbered row blocks point "down."

Sew blocks together into rows, matching seams at points indicated by black arrows in diagram above. Press seams in adjacent rows in opposite directions.

Sewing Rows Together

Sew block rows together matching seams (see small arrows in the diagram). Press seams up or down.

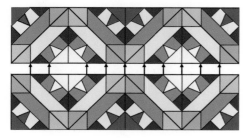

Adding Border 1

Sew Border 1 strips to the sides. Press seams toward Border 1. Sew strips to the top and bottom of the quilt. Press toward Border 1.

Adding Border 2

Add Border 2 as for Border 1.

Adding Pieced Border 3*

Painlessly Paper-Piece thirty-two *(forty)* border blocks (Z-Sections).

Sew nine *(eleven)* border blocks together to make one long strip. Make a second strip. Press seams open.

Sew seven *(nine)* border blocks together to make one long strip. Press seams open. Add 2½" print cornerstone squares to each end of the strip and press toward squares. Make a second strip.

Sew pieced (side) borders to the sides of the quilt top. Press toward Border 2. Sew pieced borders to top and bottom. Press toward Border 2.

*Detailed instructions for adjusting sizes for pieced borders are in *Quilters' General Information* on page 84.

Adding Border 4

Add Border 4 as for Border 1. Press toward Border 4.

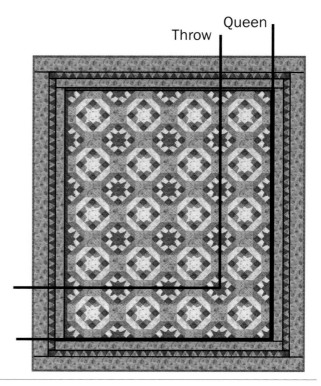

Throw

Queen

Su-Lin (Panda Bear)

Crib 50½" x 61½"

Marjorie Rhine, 2005, Damascus, Oregon

Su-Lin (Panda Bear)   Intermediate

Blocks

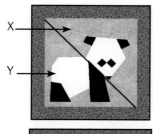

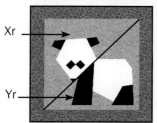

Finished Size: 9" x 9"
Each block has
two sections
and a block frame

Fabric Requirements (In yards unless specified)

	Fabric	Description	Crib 50½" x 61½" 12 blocks	Twin 67" x 78" 20 blocks
	A	Various Tone-on-Tone Prints for Block Background & Sashing	6 FQ*	10 FQ*
	B	Black	⅝	½
	C	White	¾	¾
	D	Medium Green for Framing Strips and Borders 1 & 3	1⅞	2⅞
	E	Yellow print for Sashing Cornerstones & Border 2	⅞	1⅛
		Binding	½	⅝
		Backing	3⅜ horizontal seams	4⅞ vertical seams
		Batting	57" x 68"	73" x 84"

*FQ means Fat Quarter

Cutting Strips, Sashing, Borders and Binding

Fabric	Piece	Shape	Crib # to Cut	Crib Strip Size	Twin # to Cut	Twin Strip Size
A See FQ Cutting on next page	Sashing	2½" x 9½"	31 (5 from each FQ + one more from one FQ)	See FQ Cutting	50 (5 from each FQ, one is extra)	See FQ Cutting
	X8 & X9 Strips	1¾" x 3¼"	2 from each FQ	See FQ Cutting	2 from each FQ	See FQ Cutting
B	X5 Strip	Partial Strip	1@ 16" x 1"	1"	1 @ 26" x 1"	1"
	X8 & X9 Strips	1¼" x 3¼"	12 from 1 strip**	1¼"	20 from 2 strips**	1¼"
C	X5 Strip	Partial Strip	2 @ 16" x 1¼"	1¼"	2 @ 26" x 1¼"	1¼"
D	Framing Strips	1½" x 7½"	24 from 5 strips**	1½"	40 from 8 strips**	1½"
	Framing Strips	1½" x 9½"	24 from 6 strips**	1½"	40 from 10 strips**	1½"
	Border 1	WOF Strip	5	1½"	6	1½"
	Border 3	WOF Strip	6	4½"	8	6½"
E	Border 2	WOF Strip	5	3¼"	7	4"
	Sashing Cornerstones	2½" x 2½"	20 from 2 strips**	2½"	30 from 2 strips**	2½"
	Binding	WOF Strip	7	2¼"	8	2¼"

**First cut the WOF strips, then cut the number of pieces indicated.

Cutting Patches for Paper Piecing

Fabric	Patch Name(s)		Total number of EACH in quilt	
	Panda X & Y	**Reverse Panda Xr & Yr**	**Crib**	**Twin**
 A	X10, X11, X12, X13 Y1, Y6, Y7, Y8, Y9, Y10	Xr10, Xr11, Xr12, Xr13, Yr1, Yr6, Yr7, Yr8, Yr9, Yr10	6	10
B	X1, X4, Y3, Y5	Xr1, Xr4 Yr3, Yr5	6	10
C	X2, X3, X6, X7 Y2, Y4	Xr2, Xr3, Xr6, Xr7 Yr2, Yr4	6	10

Fat Quarter (FQ) Cutting

Sashing, strips X8, X9 and background patches for one Panda and one Reverse Panda block can be cut from each Fat Quarter. Fold the FQ in half, **right sides together,** along the long edge. Follow the diagram to lay out the X- and Y-Section cutting guides and cut background patches. Cut sashing from same FQ as shown. The Xr and Yr patches will be those facing right side up after cutting.

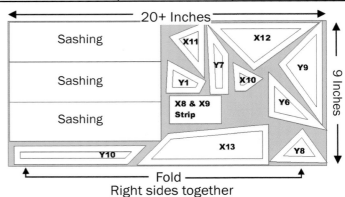

Making the Blocks (Numbers for Twin quilt in parentheses)

Preparing Pieced Unit Patch X5

Sew a white X5 strip to each side of the black X5 strip. Press toward black strip. Cross cut into twelve *(twenty)* 1¼" segments. Place in a bag labeled X5/Xr5. The same pieced patch is used for X5 and Xr5.

Pieced Unit Patch X5 and Xr5

Preparing Pieced Unit Patches X8 and X9

Sew each background X8/X9 strip to a black X8/X9 strip. Press toward black strip. Cross cut two 1½" segments from each strip set for a total of twenty-four *(forty)* 1½" segments. Place in a bag labelled X8/Xr8/X9/Xr9. The same pieced patch is used for X8, Xr8, X9 and Xr9.

Pieced Unit Patch X8, X9, Xr8 and Xr9

Piecing the Sections

Painlessly Paper-Piece six *(ten)* X-Sections, six *(ten)* Xr-Sections, six *(ten)* Y-Sections, and six *(ten)* Yr-Sections. When paper-piecing Pieced Unit Patches X5, X8 and X9 into the block, align pieced unit seamline with the seamline printed on the pattern. See detailed directions on page 57.

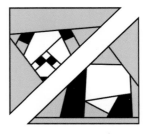

Sewing the Panda Units

Sew an X-Section to a Y-Section. There are no match points in these blocks. Press seams open. Make six *(ten)* Panda blocks. Sew an Xr-Section to a Yr-Section. Press seams open. Make six *(ten)* Reverse Panda blocks.

Adding the Framing Strips

Sew 1½" x 7½" Fabric D Framing Strips to the sides of the unit. Press toward Framing Strip. Sew 1½" x 9½" Fabric D Framing Strips to the top and bottom of the unit. Press toward Framing Strip. Make twelve *(twenty)*.

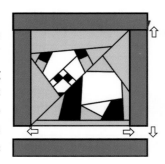

Lining up Pieced Unit Patch with Paper-Piecing Pattern

Prepare the pattern by folding back on the "next" sewing line (for patch X5, X8 or X9—whichever patch is next). Place the pieced unit patch right side up on the table. On the back of the pattern, locate the line(s) that represents the seamline(s) between the areas to be covered by the pieced patch.

Pick up the pattern with attached fabric patches and place it over the pieced patch so that the pattern seamline lines up with the seam of the pieced patch. Stitch and press.

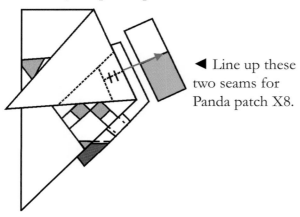

◄ Line up these two seams for Panda patch X8.

Line up these ► seams for Panda patch X5.

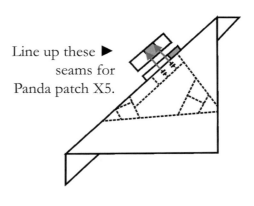

Assembling the Quilt Top

Sewing the Block Rows

Arrange blocks as desired in four *(five)* rows of three *(four)* blocks each. Sew a row of blocks together alternating blocks with Sashing Strips, starting and ending with sashing. Press toward Sashing Strips. Repeat for all block rows.

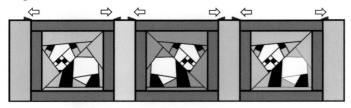

Sewing the Sashing Rows

Arrange remaining Sashing Strips as desired in five *(six)* rows of three *(four)* Sashing Strips each. Sew a row of sashing together, alternating Sashing Strips with Sashing Cornerstones, starting and ending with cornerstones. Press toward Sashing Strips.

Sewing the Rows Together

Sew alternating block rows and sashing rows together, starting and ending with a sashing row. Match block seams with cornerstone seams. Press seams either up or down.

Adding Border 1

Sew Border 1 strips to the sides. Press seams toward Border 1. Sew strips to the top and bottom of the quilt. Press toward Border 1.

Adding Borders 2 and 3

Add Borders 2 and 3 in order, following instructions for Border 1. Always press toward border just added.

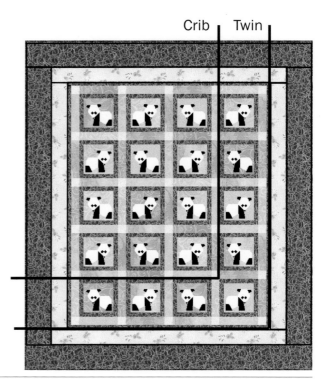

Flower Boxes

Throw 55" x 67"

Marjorie Rhine, 2005, Damascus, Oregon
Quilted by Kay Oft, Damascus, Oregon

Flower Boxes   # Advanced

Blocks

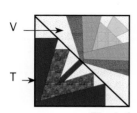

Block 1
Finished Size: 7" x 7"

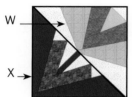

Block 2
Finished Size: 7" x 7"
Each flower block
has two sections

Setting Block
Finished Size: 7" x 7"

Fabric Requirements (In yards unless specified)

Fabric		Description	Throw 55" x 67" 12 blocks	Queen 80" x 92" 20 blocks
	A	Bright Golden Yellow	⅛	¼
	B	Medium Light Purple	⅜	⅜
	C	Medium Purple for Blocks, Framing Strips & Border 1	1	1⅝
	D	Medium Dark Purple for Blocks & Border 4	1	2¼
	E	Medium Green	¼	⅜
	F	Dark Green	⅝	⅞
	G	Light Background for Blocks, Sashing & Border 2	1⅞	3⅛
	H	Light Floral for Setting Blocks & Border 3	1	1⅞
		Binding	⅝	¾
		Backing	3⅝ horizontal seams	7⅜ horizontal seams
		Batting	61" x 73"	86" x 98"

Cutting Strips, Sashing, Borders and Binding

Fabric	Piece	Shape	Throw		Queen	
			# to Cut	Strip Size	# to Cut	Strip Size
C	Border 1	WOF Strip	5	2"	6	2½"
	Framing Strips	1½" x 10½"	4 from 2 strips*	1½"	4 from 2 strips*	1½"
	Framing Strips	1½" x 8"	20 from 4 strips*	1½"	28 from 6 strips*	1½"
	Framing Strips	1½" x 7½"	12 from 3 strips*	1½"	24 from 5 strips*	1½"
	Framing Strips	1½" x 5½"	12 from 2 strips*	1½"	24 from 4 strips*	1½"
G	Border 2	WOF Strip	6	3"	7	3¾"
	Sashing	2" x 11½"	4 from 2 strips*	2"	4 from 2 strips*	2"
	Sashing	2" x 9½"	10 from 3 strips*	2"	14 from 4 strips*	2"
	Sashing	2" x 7½"	12 from 3 strips*	2"	24 from 5 strips*	2"
	Long Sashing Strips	WOF Strip	6	2"	7	2"

*First cut the WOF strips, then cut the number of pieces indicated.

(...table continued on next page)

Cutting Strips, Borders, Setting Triangles and Binding (continued)

Fabric	Piece	Shape	Throw		Queen	
			# to Cut	Strip Size	# to Cut	Strip Size
D	Border 4	WOF Strip	7	3½"	9	6½"
H	Border 3	WOF Strip	6	3"	8	5¼"
	Side Triangles	⊠ 8⅜" QST *	10 from 3 squares	n/a	14 from 4 squares	n/a
	Corner Triangles	◺ 4½" HST **	4 from 2 squares	n/a	4 from 2 squares	n/a
	Setting Square	5½" square	6 from 1 strip***	5½"	12 from 2 strips***	5½"
	Binding	WOF Strip	7	2¼"	10	2¼"

*QST means Quarter Square Triangle
**HST means Half Square Triangle
***First cut the WOF strips, then cut the number of pieces indicated.

Cutting Patches for Paper Piecing

Fabric	Patch Name(s)	Total number of EACH in quilt	
		Throw	Queen
A	V2, W2	6	10
B	V5, W5, W6	6	10
C	V6, V7	6	10
D	W3, W4, V8, V9	6	10
E	T4, T5, X4, X5	6	10

Fabric	Patch Name(s)	Total number of EACH in quilt	
		Throw	Queen
F	T2, T8, T9, X2, X8, X9	6	10
G	T1, T3, T6, T7, T10, T11, V1, V3, V4, V10, V11, W1, W7, W8, X1, X3, X6, X7	6	10

Making the Blocks (Numbers for Queen quilt in parentheses)

Piecing the Sections

Painlessly Paper-Piece six *(ten)* T-Sections, six *(ten)* V-Sections, six *(ten)* W-Sections and six *(ten)* X-Sections.

Sewing Block 1

Sew a T-Section to a V-Section matching the stem to the center of the flower base. Press seam open. Make six *(ten)* blocks.

Sewing Block 2

Sew a W-Section to an X-Section matching the stem to the center of the flower base. Press seam open. Make six *(ten)* blocks.

Sewing the Setting Blocks

Sew 1½" x 5½" Framing Strips to the sides of a Fabric H 5½" Setting Square. Press seams toward Framing Strips.

Sew 1½" x 7½" Framing Strips to the top and bottom of the Setting Square. Press seams toward Framing Strips. Make six *(twelve)*.

Sew 2" x 7½" Sashing Strips to sides of a Setting Block. Press toward sashing. Make six *(twelve)*.

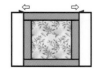

Making the Blocks (continued)

Sewing the Corner Setting Triangles

Center and sew one 1½" x 10½" Framing Strip to the long side of a Fabric H Corner Triangle. Press toward Framing Strip. Trim ends of strip.

Repeat the process using 2" x 11½" Sashing Strip. Press toward Sashing Strip. Make four.

Sewing Side Setting Triangles

Sew 1½" x 8" Framing Strips to two short sides of a Fabric H Side Triangle. Press seams toward Framing Strips. Trim ends of strips. Make ten *(fourteen)* units.

Sew 2" x 9½" Sashing Strip to the upper left side of a Side Setting Triangle unit. Press toward Sashing Strip. Trim "pointed" end parallel to opposite side. Make six *(eight)*.

Sew 2" x 9½" Sashing Strip to the upper right side of a Side Setting Triangle unit. Press toward Sashing Strip. Trim "pointed" end parallel to opposite side. Make four *(six)*.

Assembling the Quilt Top

Sewing the Block Rows

Referring to the layout diagrams on page 62, arrange blocks in six *(eight)* diagonal rows, alternating Flower Blocks with Setting Blocks. Start and end each row with Side Setting Triangles or Corner Setting Triangles according to diagram. Pay special attention to the *orientation* of the Side Setting Triangles. Sew blocks together into rows. Press seams toward sashing strips on Setting Blocks and Triangles.

Note: After sewing Side Setting Triangles or Corner Setting Triangles onto a row of blocks, the points of the sashing might hang out beyond the edge of the block. Trim the points in line with the block row.

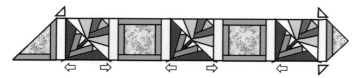

Adding Sashing Strips

Measure the length of a flower block row along the bottom edge where the sashing strip is to be sewn. Add 5" to the measurement and cut a long sashing strip of this length.

Center the sashing strip on the bottom edge of the row and sew. Press toward sashing. Trim excess sashing. Repeat for all block rows.

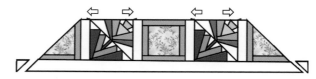

Note: Corner Setting Triangles already have sashing rows attached to them so no more sashing is required.

Sewing Rows Together

Following layout shown on next page, sew together block rows with sashing strips attached.

Adding Border 1

Sew Border 1 strips to the sides. Press seams toward Border 1. Sew strips to the top and bottom of the quilt. Press toward Border 1.

Adding Borders 2, 3 and 4

Add Borders 2, 3 and 4 in order, following instructions for Border 1. Always press toward the border just added.

Throw Quilt Layout

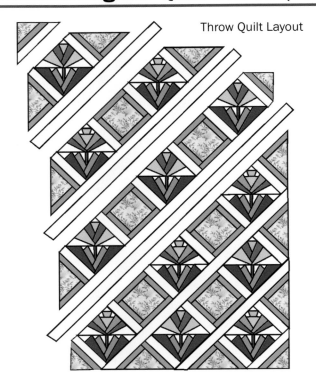

Queen Quilt Layout

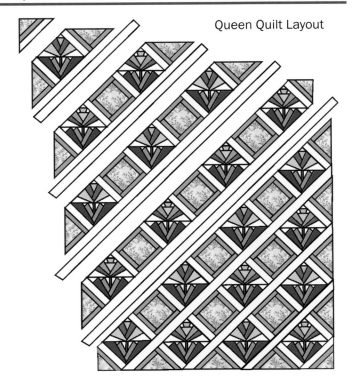

☞ *Tip!* **Aligning Sashed Rows**

When working with sashed blocks and rows that don't have cornerstones (the squares usually found between block sashing), it is easy for the block rows to become misaligned, leaving the rows looking crooked.

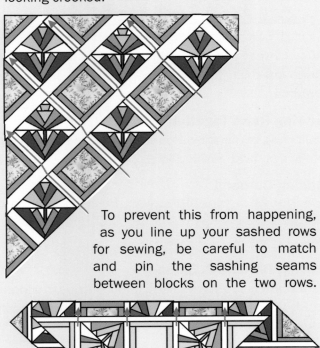

To prevent this from happening, as you line up your sashed rows for sewing, be careful to match and pin the sashing seams between blocks on the two rows.

Throw Queen

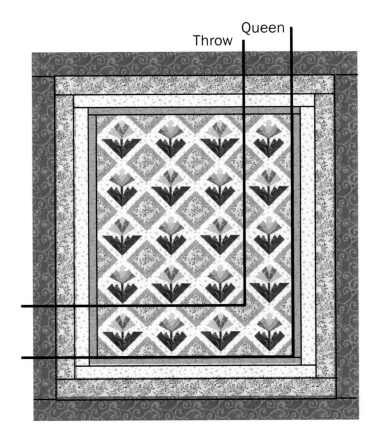

Friendly Connections

Twin 66" x 86"

Marjorie Rhine, 2005, Damascus, Oregon

Friendly Connections

Advanced

Blocks

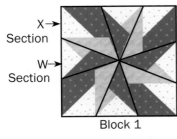

X →
Section

W →
Section

Block 1

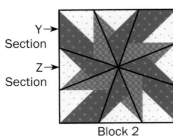

Y →
Section

Z →
Section

Block 2

Finished Block Size: 10" x 10"
Each block has 8 sections.
Block 1: 4 Each X and Y
Block 2: 4 Each W and Z
Blocks 1 & 2 are mirror images
of each other.

Fabric Requirements (In yards unless specified)

Fabric		Description	Crib 52" x 62" 12 blocks	Twin 66" x 86" 24 blocks
	A	Various Yellow Prints for Blocks & Pieced Border	3 FQ*	6 FQ*
	B	Various Red Prints for Blocks & Pieced Border	3 FQ*	6 FQ*
	C	Blue for Blocks, Pieced Border & Border 4	2⅛	4
	D	Light Background for Blocks and Borders 1 & 3	1¾	2½
		Binding	½	⅝
		Batting	58" x 68"	72" x 92"
		Backing	3⅜ horizontal seams	5¼ vertical seams

*FQ means Fat Quarter

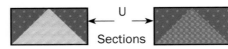

← U →

Sections

Border Blocks
Finished Size: 2½" x 5"

Cutting Cornerstones, Borders and Binding

Fabric		Piece	Shape	Crib		Twin	
				# to Cut	Strip Size	# to Cut	Strip Size
	C	Border 4	WOF Strip	6	4½"	8	6½"
		Pieced Border Cornerstone	3" Square	4 from 1 strip**	3"	4 from 1 strip**	3"
	D	Border 1	WOF Strip	4	3"	6	3"
		Border 3	WOF Strip	6	2½"	7	2½"
		Binding	WOF Strip	7	2¼"	9	2¼"

**First cut the WOF strips, then cut the number of squares indicated.

Cutting Patches for Paper Piecing

Fabric		Patch Name(s)	Total number of EACH in quilt	
			Crib	Twin
	A***	X1, W3	24	48
		U1	16	22
	B***	Y3, Z2	24	48
		U1	16	22

Fabric		Patch Name(s)	Total number of EACH in quilt	
			Crib	Twin
	C	W2, X3, Y1, Z3	24	48
		U2, U3	32	44
	D	W1, X2, Y2, Z1	24	48

***See Fat Quarter Cutting on next page

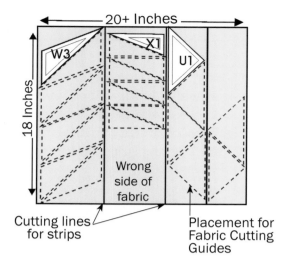

20+ Inches

18 Inches

W3   X1   U1

Wrong side of fabric

Cutting lines for strips

Placement for Fabric Cutting Guides

Fat Quarter (FQ) Cutting

Patches for two pinwheel blocks and up to six border blocks can be cut from each Fabric A and Fabric B fat quarter. The diagram shows how to cut Fabric A strips and how to place fabric guides for cutting yellow patches for Block 1 and yellow Border Blocks. First cut the fabric strips, then position Fabric Cutting Guides and cut patches. To further speed up cutting, layer multiple yellow FQs **all right sides down**, then cut using fabric guides against wrong side of the fabric. *Note:* The diagram shows cutting for yellow FQs. The same diagram can be used for cutting red FQ patches which are mirrors of the yellow. However, place Fabric Cutting Guides on **right side** of red fabric and cut from **right side**.

Making the Blocks (Numbers for Twin Quilt in parentheses)

Piecing the Sections

Painlessly Paper-Piece twenty-four *(forty-eight)* of each of the block sections (W, X, Y, Z).

Sewing Block 1

Sew each X-Section to a W-Section. There are no seams to match when sewing these sections together. Press the seam open.

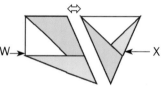

W→   ←X

Sew four W/X units together to make a block. The only match point is the center of the block. Press seams open as you go. Make six *(twelve)* blocks.

Sewing Block 2

Sew each Y-Section to a Z-Section as described for Block 1. Press seams open.

Z→   ←Y

Sew four Y/Z units together to make a block. Press seams open as you go. Make six *(twelve)* blocks.

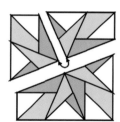

Tip!

To properly align the sections when sewing an X-Section to a W-section (Block 1) or a Y-Section to a Z-Section (Block 2), place the X-Section on top of the W-Section (Z-Section on top of the Y-Section) with points and long edges of the sections aligned. Pin the points to keep them together. Stitch from the edge of the sections toward the point.

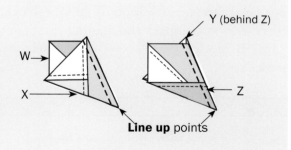

W→   Y (behind Z)

X→   ←Z

Line up points

Assembling the Quilt Top

Sewing the Block Rows

Referring to the quilt diagram at the bottom right, lay out the blocks in four (*six*) rows of three (*four*) blocks each. Blocks within a row will alternate between Block 1 and Block 2. Odd-numbered rows will start with Block 1, even-numbered rows start with Block 2. Sew blocks together into rows matching seams (see black arrows in diagram). Press seams open.

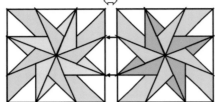

Sewing Rows Together

Sew rows together matching seams at points indicated by arrows in diagram. Press seams open.

Adding Border 1

Sew Border 1 strips to the sides. Press seams toward Border 1. Sew strips to the top and bottom of the quilt. Press toward Border 1.

Adding Pieced Border 2*

Painlessly Paper-Piece sixteen (*twenty-two*) border blocks using U1 patches in Fabric A and sixteen (*twenty-two*) U1 patches in Fabric B.

For side borders, sew nine (*thirteen*) border blocks together, alternating Fabric B border blocks with Fabric A border blocks and starting and ending with Fabric B blocks. Press seams open. Make two side border strips.

Sew pieced borders to the sides of the quilt top. Press seams toward Border 1.

For top border, sew seven (*nine*) border blocks together, alternating Fabric A blocks with Fabric B blocks and starting and ending with Fabric A blocks. Press seams open. Sew Border Cornerstone squares to each end of the row. Make 2 border strips, one for top and one for bottom border.

Sew side pieced borders to the sides of the quilt top. Press seams toward Border 1.

Sew pieced borders to the top and bottom of the quilt. Press seams toward Border 1.

Adding Borders 3 and 4

Add Borders 3 and 4 in order, as for Border 1. Always press toward border just added.

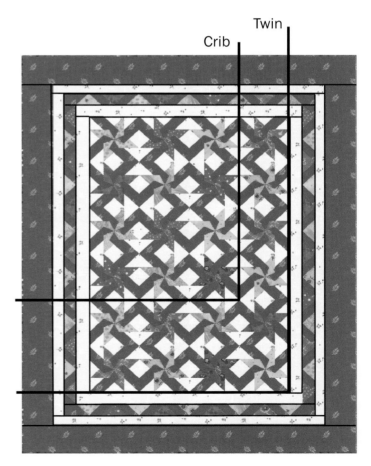

* Detailed instructions for adjusting sizes for pieced borders are in *Quilters' General Information* on page 84.

The Paper Patterns

Each paper pattern page contains the paper pattern(s) for the project named, a colored picture of the block(s) and a table showing which areas of the pattern are copies or mirrors of each other, if any.

The patterns are full-size. Make sure any copies you make are exactly the same size as those printed on these pages. You have permission to make copies of the patterns on pages 68–83 for your personal use. These patterns are copyrighted and may not be copied for others—for free or for sale.

The colored picture on each page shows the block as it would appear after it is sewn into the quilt. The paper pattern is the reverse of the final sewn block. Seam allowances are **not** shown.

Remember that as a bonus, the fabric guides for each pattern are available for free on my website: www.PainlessPaperPiecing.com. In addition, information for other sizes of the projects are on the same website. (See page 30.)

Have fun!

Treasure Star

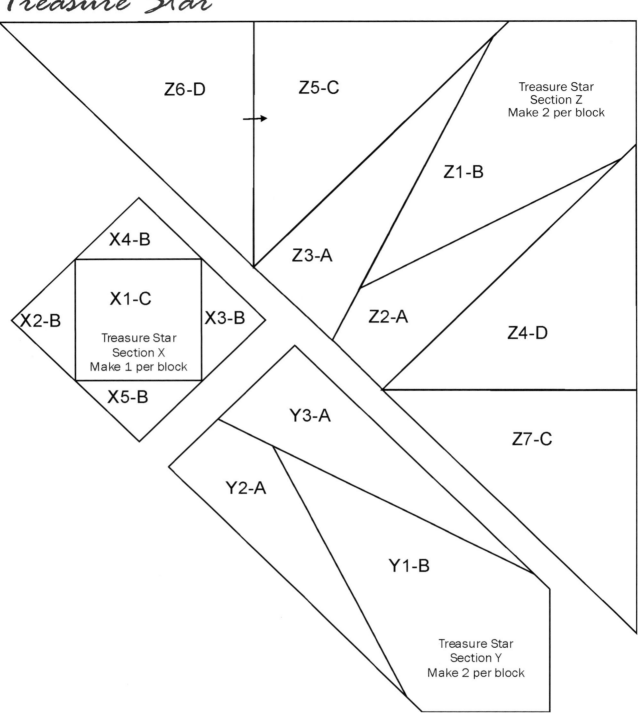

Z6-D

Z5-C

Treasure Star
Section Z
Make 2 per block

Z1-B

X4-B

X1-C

Treasure Star
Section X
Make 1 per block

X2-B

X3-B

X5-B

Z3-A

Z2-A

Z4-D

Y3-A

Z7-C

Y2-A

Y1-B

Treasure Star
Section Y
Make 2 per block

✄ Reduce the number of Fabric Guides needed by using one guide to cut multiple patches. See "Cutting Copy and Mirror Patches" on page 26.

Use Guide	To Cut Fabric Patches
X2	X2, X3, X4 and X5
Y1	Y1 and Z1
Y2	Y2 and Z2
Y3	Y3 and Z3
Z4	Z4, Z5, Z6 and Z7

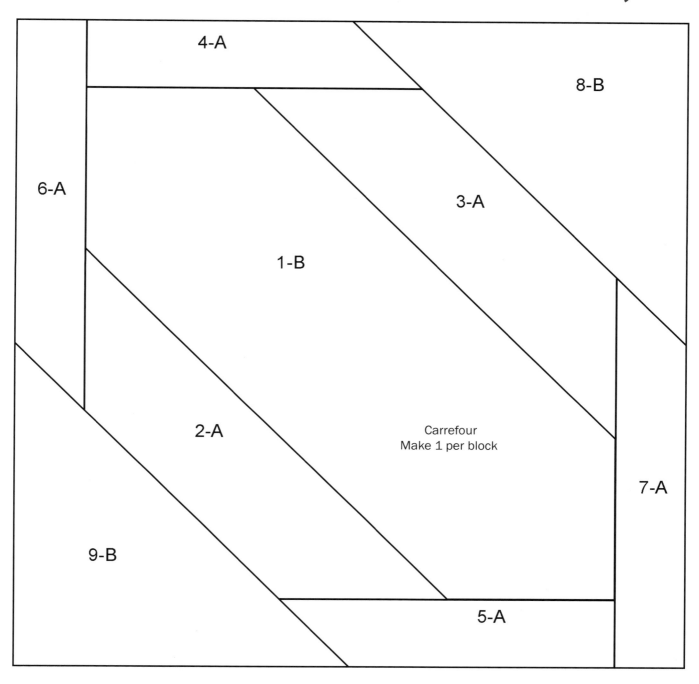

4-A

8-B

6-A

3-A

1-B

2-A

Carrefour
Make 1 per block

7-A

9-B

5-A

✄ Reduce the number of Fabric Guides needed by using one guide to cut multiple patches. See "Cutting Copy and Mirror Patches" on page 26.

Use Guide	To Cut Fabric Patches
2	2 and 3
4	4 and 5
6	6 and 7
8	8 and 9

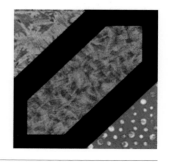

Starflower

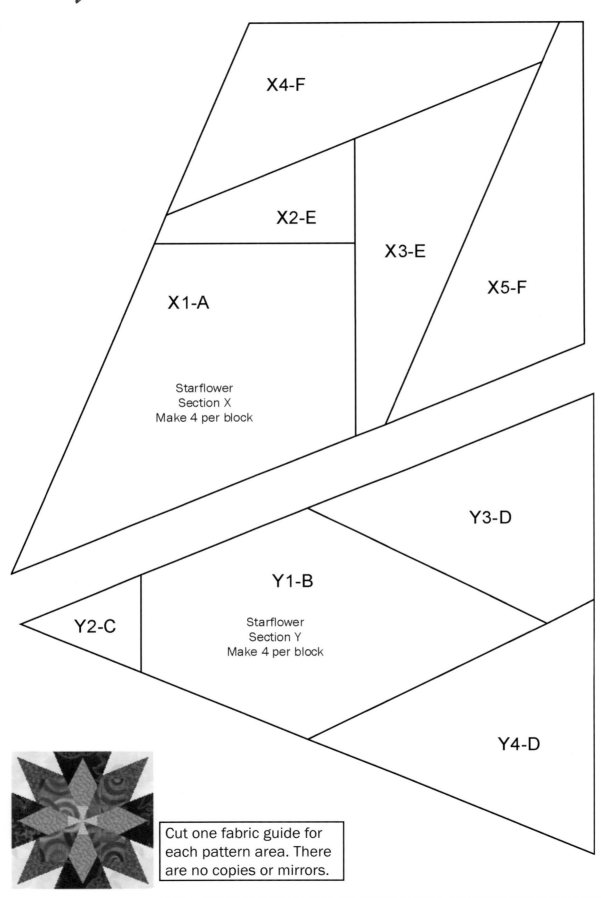

X4-F

X2-E

X3-E

X5-F

X1-A

Starflower
Section X
Make 4 per block

Y3-D

Y1-B

Y2-C

Starflower
Section Y
Make 4 per block

Y4-D

Cut one fabric guide for
each pattern area. There
are no copies or mirrors.

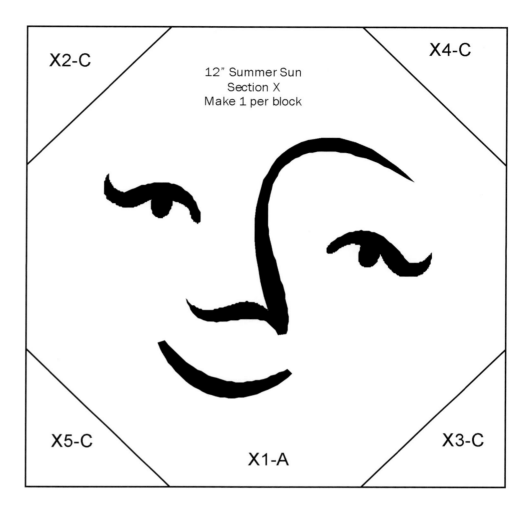

X2-C

X4-C

12" Summer Sun
Section X
Make 1 per block

X5-C

X3-C

X1-A

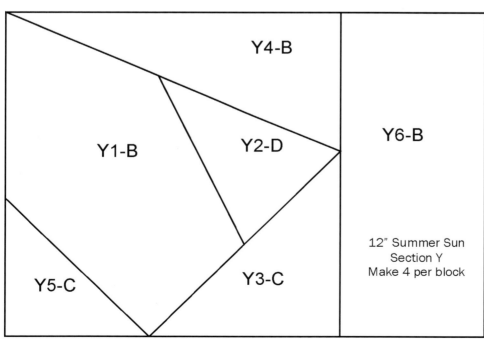

Y4-B

Y1-B

Y2-D

Y6-B

Y5-C

Y3-C

12" Summer Sun
Section Y
Make 4 per block

✄ Reduce the number of Fabric Guides needed by using one guide to cut multiple patches. See "Cutting Copy and Mirror Patches" on page 26.

Use Guide	To Cut Fabric Patches
X2	X2, X3, X4 and X5

(...continued on next page)

Summer Sun 12" *(continued)*

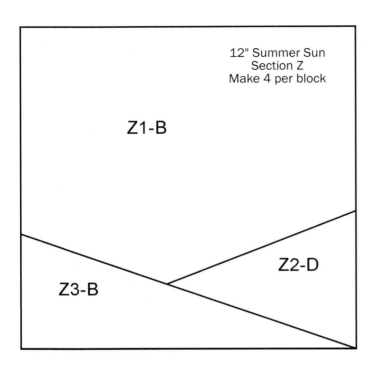

12" Summer Sun
Section Z
Make 4 per block

Z1-B

Z2-D

Z3-B

Summer Sun 5"

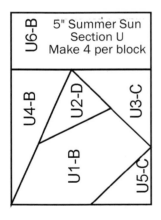

5" Summer Sun
Section U
Make 4 per block

U6-B
U4-B
U2-D
U3-C
U1-B
U5-C

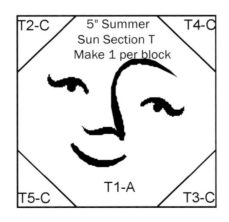

T2-C
5" Summer
Sun Section T
Make 1 per block
T4-C
T5-C
T1-A
T3-C

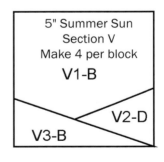

5" Summer Sun
Section V
Make 4 per block

V1-B
V2-D
V3-B

✂ *For 5" Summer Sun*
Reduce the number of Fabric Guides needed by using one guide to cut multiple patches. See "Cutting Copy and Mirror Patches" on page 26.

Use Guide	To Cut Fabric Patches
T2	T2, T3, T4 and T5

Su Lin (Panda Bear)

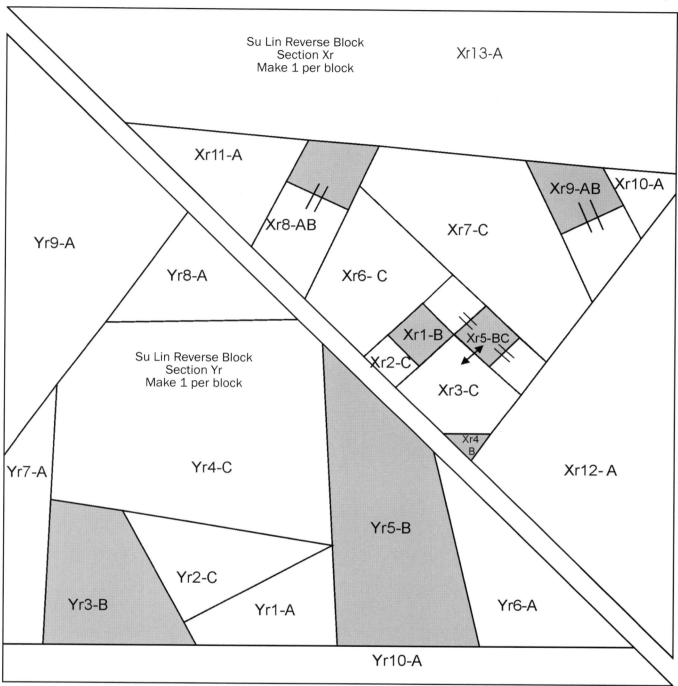

Su Lin Reverse Block
Section Xr
Make 1 per block

Xr13-A

Xr11-A

Xr9-AB

Xr10-A

Yr9-A

Xr8-AB

Xr7-C

Yr8-A

Xr6- C

Xr1-B

Xr5-BC

Xr2-C

Su Lin Reverse Block
Section Yr
Make 1 per block

Xr3-C

Xr4 B

Yr7-A

Yr4-C

Xr12- A

Yr5-B

Yr2-C

Yr3-B

Yr1-A

Yr6-A

Yr10-A

Su-Lin Reverse Block

Flower Boxes Block 1

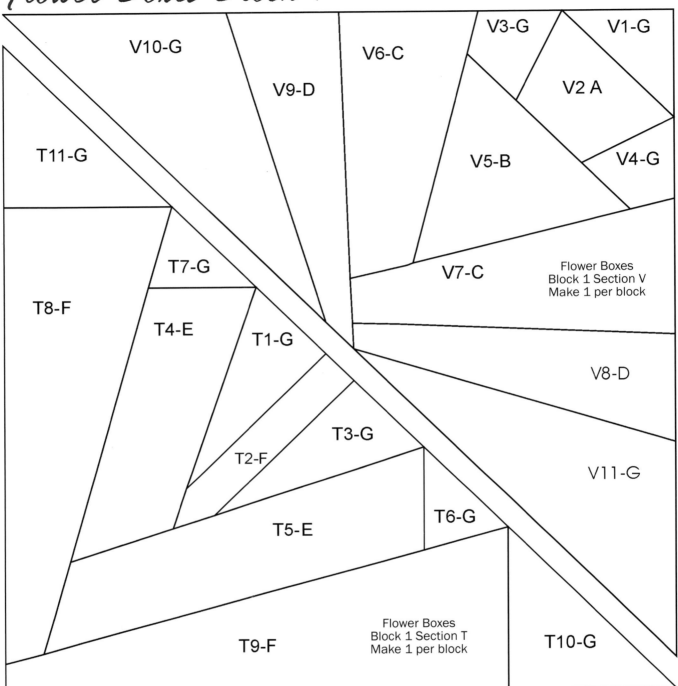

V10-G

V3-G

V1-G

V6-C

V9-D

V2 A

T11-G

V5-B

V4-G

V7-C

Flower Boxes
Block 1 Section V
Make 1 per block

T7-G

T8-F

T4-E

T1-G

V8-D

T3-G

T2-F

V11-G

T5-E

T6-G

Flower Boxes
Block 1 Section T
Make 1 per block

T9-F

T10-G

Flower Box
Block 1

✂ Reduce the number of Fabric Guides needed by using one guide to cut multiple patches. See "Cutting Copy and Mirror Patches" on page 26.

Use Guide	To Cut Fabric Patches
V1	V1 and W1
V3	V3 and mirror or reverse patch V4
T1	T1 and X1; and mirror or reverse patches T3 and X3
T2	T2 and X2
T4	T4 and X4
T5	T5 and X5
T6	T6 and X6; and mirror or reverse patches T7 and X7
T10	T10 and T11

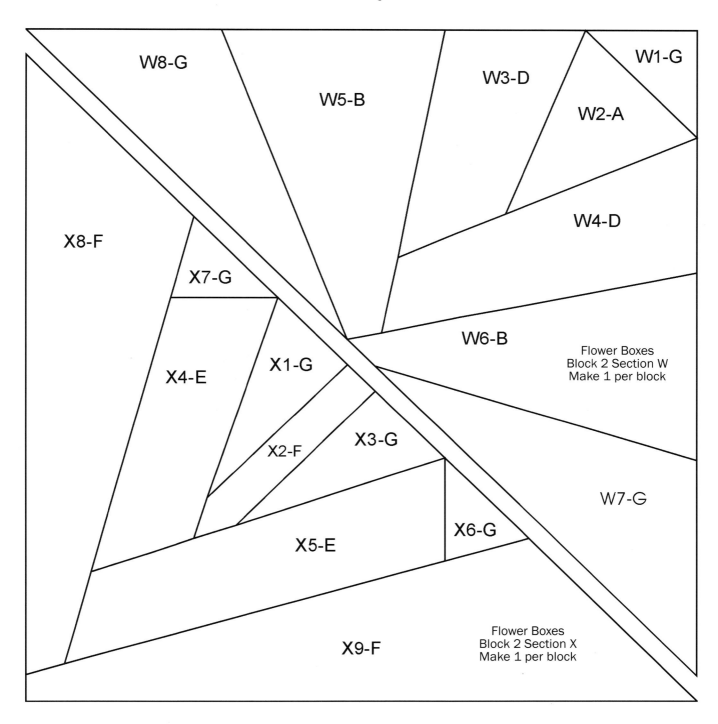

W8-G

W5-B

W3-D

W1-G

W2-A

W4-D

X8-F

X7-G

W6-B

Flower Boxes
Block 2 Section W
Make 1 per block

X4-E

X1-G

X2-F

X3-G

W7-G

X5-E

X6-G

X9-F

Flower Boxes
Block 2 Section X
Make 1 per block

Flower Box
Block 2

Friendly Connections Block 1

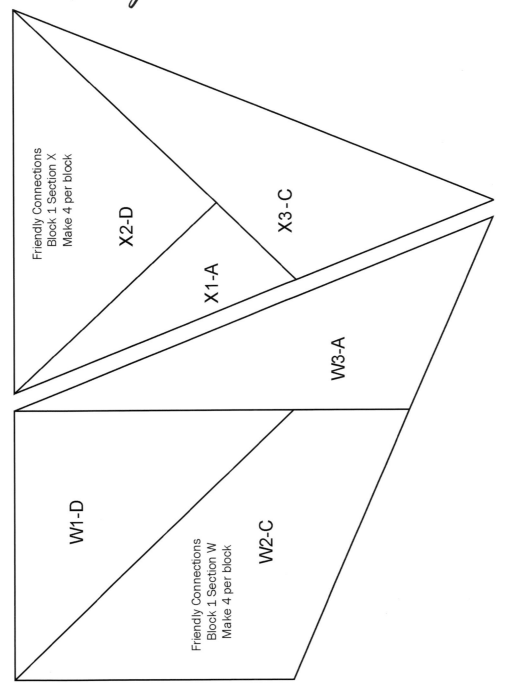

Friendly Connections
Block 1 Section X
Make 4 per block

X2-D

X3-C

X1-A

W3-A

W1-D

Friendly Connections
Block 1 Section W
Make 4 per block

W2-C

Block 1

✂ Reduce the number of Fabric Guides needed by using one guide to cut multiple patches. See "Cutting Copy and Mirror Patches" on page 26.	
Use Guide	To Cut Fabric Patches
Each W-Section guide	W-Section patches & Y-Section patches of the same number
Each X-Section guide	X-Section patches & Z-Section patches of the same number (W & X section patches in Block 1 are mirrors or reverses of the same numbered patches in Y & Z sections in Block 2.)
U2	U2 and U3 border block patches (pattern on next page)

Friendly Connections Block 2

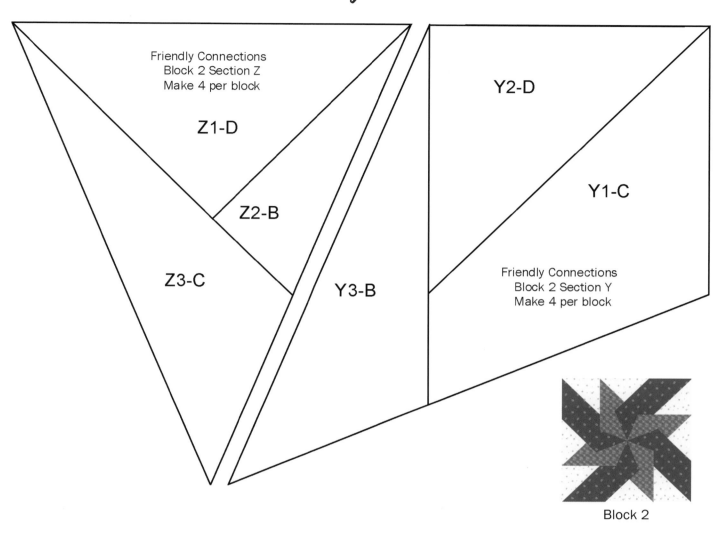

Friendly Connections
Block 2 Section Z
Make 4 per block

Z1-D

Z2-B

Z3-C

Y3-B

Y2-D

Y1-C

Friendly Connections
Block 2 Section Y
Make 4 per block

Block 2

Friendly Connections Border Block

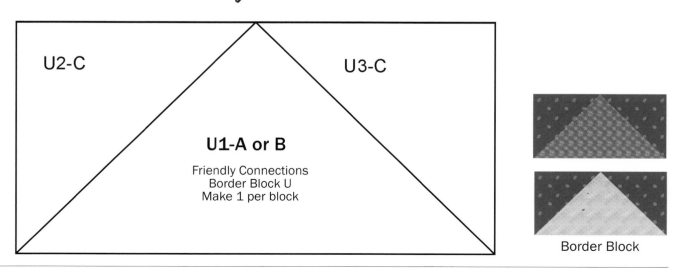

U2-C

U3-C

U1-A or B

Friendly Connections
Border Block U
Make 1 per block

Border Block

Borders

All borders for projects in this book, except pieced borders, are applied in the same way. Sew border strips together to make one long strip. Cutting directions include enough fabric for diagonal seams.

Place border strips **right sides together** with the bottom strip horizontal and the top strip vertical. Draw a diagonal line from the left corner of the top strip to the point where it intersects with the bottom strip. Sew **on** the line and trim seam allowance to ¼". Press to one side.

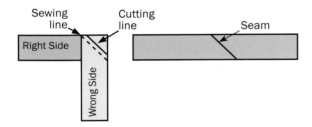

Measure the length of quilt top from top to bottom, through the center of the quilt. Cut two border strips this length. Fold these side border strips in half, then half again to find center and quarter points for the borders. Mark points on strips with creases or pins. Repeat to find center and quarter points of quilt top. Matching ends, centers and quarter points, pin the borders to the sides of the quilt, easing as necessary. Sew, then press seams toward new borders.

Measure the width of quilt top through its center including the added side borders. Cut two border strips this length. Fold border strips in half, then half again to find center and quarter points. Mark with creases or pins. Repeat to find center and quarter points of quilt top. Matching ends, center and quarter-points, pin the borders to the top and bottom of the quilt. Sew, then press seams toward new borders.

Adjusting Pieced Borders

If all sewing is precise the pieced borders will fit perfectly to the quilt. However, not all quilters can sew a perfect ¼" seam allowance so a pieced border might be a bit too large or too small and may need to be adjusted.

Prepare the quilt up to making the pieced border. Construct the pieced borders for all sides of the quilt. If a pieced border calls for cornerstones, do **not** add the cornerstones until the border is adjusted to fit.

Side Borders

Measure the quilt top from top to bottom, through the middle of the quilt and record the measurement. Measure the length of the pieced borders you made for the sides of the quilt.

If the borders are the same length as the quilt top (or very close!) no adjustment is necessary.

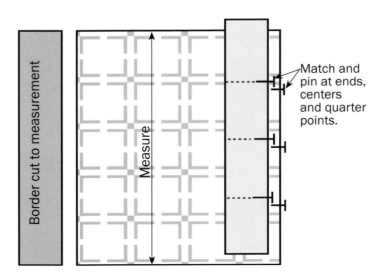

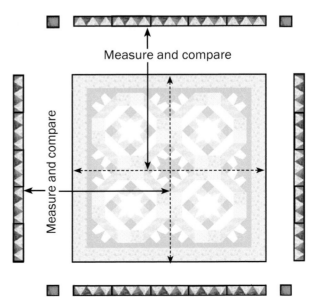

If pieced border is too long

Resew seams between pieced border blocks using a bigger seam allowance until the border is the same length as the quilt top.

If border is too short

If the border is shorter than the quilt top by only a small amount (1" or less), resew seams between pieced border blocks taking a slightly smaller seam allowance until the border is the same length as the quilt top.

If the border is shorter by more than one inch, cut two small pieces the same width and same fabric as used for cornerstones—do not cut the cornerstone itself. Sew one piece to each end of the pieced border. Measure the border and trim to fit—it is best to trim equal amounts from each end of the pieced border.

Lengthen border by adding patches

Check the length for the second side border and adjust if necessary. Do not sew the borders to the quilt yet.

Top and Bottom Borders

Measure the quilt top from side to side, through the middle of the quilt and record the measurement. Measure the length of the pieced border for the top of the quilt.

If the top border needs adjustment to fit, follow previous instructions as for side border. Repeat the process for the bottom border.

Add Cornerstones and Sew Border

Sew cornerstones to each end of the top and bottom pieced borders.

Sew the side borders to the sides of the quilt then sew the top and bottom borders to the quilt. Press according to the quilt project instructions.

Backing

The quilt backing should be cut at least 6" wider and longer than the quilt top. Small projects such as placemats and tablerunners need only 4" extra width and length. Piece the back as necessary and press the seams open. To avoid puckers, be sure to remove fabric selvedges before sewing backing pieces together. Fabric requirements for larger projects in this book specify either vertical or horizontal seam(s) for the backing.

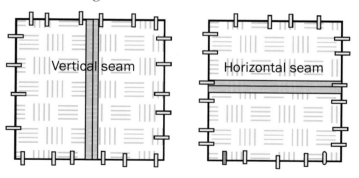

Basting for Quilting

Mark the quilt top for quilting.

Right side down, place the backing on a large flat surface. Pull the back taut and tape down to hold in place. Center the batting on the quilt back and smooth from the center out. Center the quilt top, **right side up,** on the batting.

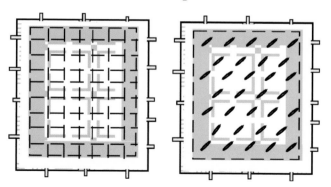

Starting at the center of the quilt, baste the three layers together. Basting can be done by hand, with safety pins, a basting gun, temporary fabric adhesive spray or other method. Basting lines, pins, etc. should be about 4" apart. Thread baste around the outside edge of the quilt.

After the quilt is quilted, remove all remaining basting pins and threads, except for the basting around the outside edge of the quilt. Trim batting and backing even with the edge of the quilt top.

Binding

Using a diagonal seam (see page 84), sew binding strips together to make one long strip. Press seams open. Cut the first end at a 45° angle. Fold the binding in half by hand, **wrong sides together**, along the first 12" of long raw edges.

Trim end

Near the midpoint on one edge of the front of the quilt, place two pins 10" apart. Starting at the center point between the pins, lay the folded binding strip on the quilt top aligning the raw edges of the binding with the edge of the quilt. Starting at the second pin, sew the binding to the quilt, folding the binding **wrong sides together** as you sew. Use a ¼" seam. Stop at ¼" from the quilt corner. Backstitch, remove from machine and cut threads.

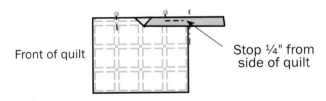
Front of quilt
Stop ¼" from side of quilt

To turn the corner, first fold the binding straight up. Then bring it straight down so the fold of the binding is aligned with the top raw edge of the quilt. Start stitching at the edge of the quilt. Go forward a couple of stitches, backstitch two stitches, then stitch the length of the side until you are ¼" from the next quilt corner.

Repeat the corner fold process as you sew all sides of the quilt.

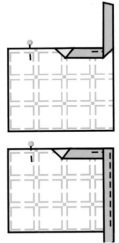

When you reach the first pin (10" from where you started stitching) backstitch and remove the quilt from the machine.

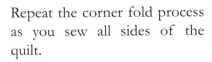

Unfold the tail end of the binding. Lift up the starting portion of the binding and position the tail (at the end of the binding) underneath it. If the tail is too long to fit under the start, trim the tail so it ends about 3" beyond the start of the binding.

Mark the position of the start of the binding on **the wrong side** of the tail with a pin or pencil line. This pin or line will be at a 45° angle.

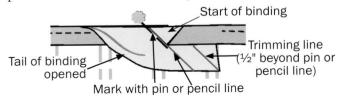
Start of binding
Trimming line (½" beyond pin or pencil line)
Tail of binding opened
Mark with pin or pencil line

Without removing the pin, trim the tail ½" beyond the pin (away from the pin **towards** the excess tail end of binding) at a 45° angle, parallel to the pin.

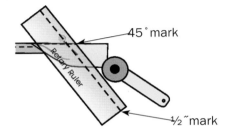
45° mark
Rotary Ruler
½" mark

Unfold the starting portion of the binding and sew the two ends **right sides together** to create a continuous strip of binding. Press seam open.

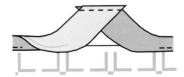

Refold the binding and place it on top of the quilt. Complete sewing the binding to the quilt. Turn the edge of the binding to the back side of the quilt and blindstitch in place by hand, folding in the excess at the corners to create mitered corners.

Back of quilt